THE
DIFFERENCE

WEALTH-BUILDING JOURNAL

—•→

Discover How *You* Can Prosper
in Even the Toughest Times

←•—

Jean Chatzky

Po

Copyright © 2009 by Jean Chatzky

All rights reserved.

Published in the United States by Potter Style, an imprint of the Crown Publishing Group,
a division of Random House, Inc., New York.

Potter Style is a trademark and Potter and colophon are registered trademarks of
Random House, Inc.

This journal is a companion to the book *The Difference: How Anyone Can Prosper in Even the Toughest
Times* by Jean Chatzky, with new material. *The Difference* was published by Crown Business,
an imprint of the Crown Publishing Group, a division of Random House, Inc., New York.

www.clarksonpotter.com
www.crownpublishing.com

ISBN 978-0-307-45286-3

Printed in the United States of America

Design by Danielle Deschenes

10 9 8 7 6 5 4 3 2 1

First Edition

What's The Difference?

There are some people who seem to possess the innate ability to rise above negative circumstances and to effortlessly ascend financial, social, and corporate ladders. They don't seem to worry about their finances. These people aren't just big-business tycoons—they're people you know: your boss, neighbors, and often, your friends.

What's the difference between you and them? Thanks to the groundbreaking research conducted for my book *The Difference*, I can tell you—and I can do it in very precise terms. A study of more than five thousand individuals conducted by Harris Interactive in cooperation with Merrill Lynch has given me the ability to tear the covers off the four groups of people who make up the new economic strata in America today. They are:

The wealthy (W)	3 percent
The financially comfortable (FC)	27 percent
The paycheck-to-paychecks (PTPs)	54 percent
The further-in-debtors (FIDs)	15 percent

Through this research, we now know that people who have achieved both financial comfort and wealth are distinctly different from those who are struggling paycheck to paycheck or sinking further into debt each month. They are different in both personality and habit. The wealthy and financially comfortable share attributes, beliefs, and behaviors that people who are living paycheck to paycheck or sinking further into debt lack.

The good news: These attributes, beliefs, and behaviors are all things you can learn. To do so, you'll need to wake up some parts of you that have been sleeping, perhaps for years, perhaps for decades. You'll need to tune in to parts of your personality and tap portions of your potential that you may not realize you have. This journal is designed to guide you through that very process: It is filled with exercises that will help you master the personality traits and habits you need in order to see The Difference in your life.

Meet the Wealthy

Only 3 percent of Americans are truly wealthy. But there is no doubt it's good to be one of them. On average, they have investable assets (not including home equity) of nearly $2 million, but we categorized them as wealthy if they had achieved significant wealth at a younger age:

$1 million or more for ages 55 or older
$750,000 or more for ages 45 to 54
$500,000 or more for ages 35 to 44
$250,000 or more if under age 35

How did they get there? What made them wealthy? I wanted specifics of which behaviors, attitudes, goals, and personality traits mattered most.

In my joining forces with Merrill Lynch and Harris Interactive, we created a survey that asked hundreds of questions grouped into four loosely constructed categories: nonfinancial behaviors, financial attitudes/behaviors, goals (both financial and life), and personality. We tested for hundreds of factors. In the end, I was able to distill twenty key factors that all wealthy participants held in common. I then divided these factors into four habits and seven personality traits. Collectively, these attributes make up The Difference.

Seven Traits of the Wealthy Personality

OPTIMISM   DRIVE   INTUITION

RESILIENCE   CURIOSITY   CONFIDENCE

CONNECTEDNESS

Four Habits of the Wealthy

HARD WORK   GIVE BACK   INVEST SOUNDLY AND AGGRESSIVELY

SAVE HABITUALLY

How to Use This Journal: A Summary of the Chapters

This journal is organized into eight chapters; each deals with one attribute or a combination of attributes that make up The Difference. It is important to note up front that these attributes rarely work independently. Having one personality trait or habit will help you develop the others. The Differences circle one another, diving in and out, weaving a nice little web that becomes a life. I encourage you, however, not to skip around; try to address the chapters in order, since each one is intended to build on the others.

That said, not every exercise will be for you—and that's because not every attribute will rank as high on your internal list of what's important. You may encounter some exercises that don't seem relevant to your life at this moment, but make a note to come back to them later. There are checklists in the beginning of each chapter so that you can check off the exercises that you've tried.

CHAPTER 1, "ATTRIBUTE FOCUS: SAVING." A fundamental part of The Difference is understanding that spending more than you make is just as bad for you emotionally as it is financially. Saving money, on the other hand, is actually good for both your health and your wealth. The wealthy get that. I'll share their strategies.

CHAPTER 2, "ATTRIBUTE FOCUS: INVESTING." Do you want to secure your financial future? Then you need to have an investment plan, take steps to bring it to life, take reasonable risks, and get help from a financial planner if and when you need it. I'll show you—step-by-step—what to do.

CHAPTER 3, "ATTRIBUTE FOCUS: DRIVE." People who fully understand The Difference identify what they want, plot a course, and succeed. Every day, they think about what's next and set about achieving it with intention and purpose. In this chapter, you'll select one financial goal and chart your own course of action. You must choose to make The Difference a part of your life.

CHAPTER 4, "ATTRIBUTE FOCUS: HARD WORK." The definition of hard work is not what it used to be. Sure, putting in the hours is often part of the process—but making the most of those hours is even more important. This chapter will explain how to use your particular skill set to do precisely that.

CHAPTER 5, "ATTRIBUTE FOCUS: PASSION AND CURIOSITY." People who know The Difference have figured out what sort of work actually makes sense for them. For them, it's not a job, it's not a career, it's a calling. Once you find your passion, you'll see that it doesn't feel like work. But while you're searching for it, you can still bring passion to your current work; this chapter will show you how to do both.

CHAPTER 6, "ATTRIBUTE FOCUS: CONNECTEDNESS." Connecting with the world and the people in it—which means putting yourself out there—is key to The Difference. If you're feeling low in social capital, in this chapter you'll discover that you have more potential connections than you think, and you'll learn how to use them.

CHAPTER 7, "ATTRIBUTE FOCUS: OPTIMISM." From the burgeoning study of positive psychology, we now know that optimists make more money, scale the career heights, have better relationships, and stay healthier longer than pessimists. Complete this chapter to boost your sense of happiness and optimism—traits that feed into almost every other aspect of The Difference.

CHAPTER 8, "ATTRIBUTE FOCUS: RESILIENCE." Many wealthy people have triumphed over dismal financial setbacks. This is the chapter that you'll turn to when things simply aren't going your way. You'll learn to pick yourself up, dust yourself off, and get back in the game.

CHAPTER 9, "ATTRIBUTE FOCUS: GRATITUDE AND GIVING BACK." Saying thanks is the ultimate karma kickback. The new science of gratitude teaches us that being grateful makes us more successful and wealthier over time. This chapter will prove that feeling truly grateful is something that we can learn—and it is also the quickest way to feel truly rich.

In the End . . .

The Difference is as much about doing as it is about believing. It's about making your own luck, not taking no for an answer, and paying attention to the things you're doing—both right and wrong—so that you can accomplish more with fewer sidesteps in the future. Believing alone won't make it happen. All the wishful thinking you can muster won't make it happen. Doing makes all The Difference in the world. That's what this journal is all about.

Writing down a goal is the first step to making it real.
Are you ready to start making your financial dreams a reality?

CHAPTER
NẸ

ATTRIBUTE FOCUS:

SAVING

Date that I began this chapter: _2_ / _9_ / _10_

Date that I completed this chapter: ____/____/____

There are two habits you must master to make The Difference in your life. The first is saving habitually; the second is investing, which we will cover in chapter 2.

The simple fact is that if you want to build wealth, you have to spend less than you make. Most people in this country are not doing this. Yet it is fairly simple to right your ship by tracking your spending and cutting out needless expenditures (big and small). This chapter will provide you with every tool you need to rediscover the lost art—and healing power—of saving money.

Exercise Checklist

❏ **Eyes on the Prize**
❏ **What I Spent in One Month**
❏ **Putting It in Perspective: The Most Important Things in Life Aren't Things**
❏ **Create a Budget**
❏ **Retirement: How Much Do You Need to Save?**

The Healing Power of Saving

Why is saving so important? Several reasons. First, without a basic savings account—an emergency cushion—you get stuck in a cycle of debt and more debt. Think about it this way: You are driving along the highway in your steady-eddy sedan. All of a sudden you notice . . . the brakes don't have the oomph that they used to. So you take it into the shop and, yes, you need new ones. If you have savings, you pull out your plastic knowing that when the bill arrives you'll pay it off immediately. But if you don't? You layer that charge atop all of those already on your credit card bill, and the cycle of revolving debt begins—making saving impossible.

Second, if you can't save, you can't invest. And investing—whether you do it in stocks or bonds, real estate or commodities, or preferably some combination of the above (again, more on this in chapter 2)—is the only way to ensure that the value of your hard-earned cash keeps pace with inflation and taxes.

Third, saving is synonymous with peace of mind. When you save money, you are taking care of yourself and everyone who depends on you. You are saying to all of those people: "You matter and so do I, and so I am going to put having money in the bank ahead of all of those 'things' that we think we want but don't actually need." I know from the research conducted for my book on financial happiness that people who manage to put away at least 5 percent of their earnings month in and month out feel significantly better than those who don't. (That may not ultimately be enough to fund your retirement, but it's a start, and once you start you will feel empowered to do more.) It is for all of these reasons that Wharton professor Robert J. Meyer described the act of saving money as "healing." I could not agree more.

And fourth and finally, saving is your only road to financial independence. If you have money saved you have power—to walk out of a bad job, a bad relationship, a bad situation. You very likely have the confidence that comes with having saved that money as well.

Why Is Saving Money So Difficult?

Saving money means making a conscious choice that you are not going to buy one thing (at a time) but are, instead, going to leave the money in your bank account—or your wallet—where it can grow into the slush fund that you will eventually invest to fund your life's dreams and goals. Sounds simple, but why is it so difficult? Choosing to save is almost always opting for delayed gratification instead of immediate gratification. The allure of getting something good today is much greater than the allure of getting something years in the future—even if the reward in the future is bigger.

Chapter 3 of this journal is devoted entirely to setting one major financial goal and practicing strategies for staying on course. But if saving for the distant future—say, for retirement—is too much of an abstraction at the moment, start off by thinking about some more immediate reasons (and immediate rewards) for saving money.

Eyes on the Prize

Think about one relatively short-term savings goal (something that you want to accomplish within the next six months). Maybe you have an upcoming expense—a vacation or some back-to-school shopping—that you want to pay for entirely in cash instead of using your credit card. Answer the following questions:

What am I saving for? _Vacation w/ MSZ_

How much does it cost? _2K_

Do I have anything saved already? _No_

How much more do I need? _2K_

How many months (or pay periods) do I have to come up with this money?
Six months (Mar - aug)

How much do I have to save each month (or pay period) to meet my goal?
350 $ / Month .

How will I benefit from saving this money? How will I feel after reaching this goal?

NOTE: The next few exercises will involve taking a close, hard look at your spending habits so that you can find the money that you want to save. These exercises can be tough, so keep thinking about your goal as you work through them.

What I Spent in One Month

The only way to save is to start tracking where your money is going today. This is a tedious exercise—I want to acknowledge that right off the bat. But you do not have to do it forever. Instead, for the next month, make a commitment to write down every dollar—every dime—that you spend and where it goes. You can do this by tucking this notebook into your bag and being diligent about taking notes. You can (as I do) get a receipt every single time you make a purchase, shove those receipts into your wallet, and log them every few days.

When you are through you'll have a road map that shows where all of your money has gone. I guarantee if you have never done this you will be surprised. You will see that more of your money is going to pet supplies or random trips to the grocery store or other nonessentials than you thought.

Date	Expense/Item Purchased	Amount

Date	Expense/Item Purchased	Amount

Date	Expense/Item Purchased	Amount

Date	Expense/Item Purchased	Amount

Date	Expense/Item Purchased	Amount

Create a Budget

Now that you have tracked your expenses for a month, use that information to fill in the blanks in the "Tracked Month" column in the budget worksheet below.

Then, fill in the blanks for the next month, indicating how much you *want* to spend on those same items (in the "New Budget" column). Some things—mortgage payments, car loans—will be fixed. For those that are variable, over which you can exercise control, start with small changes—changes you'll be able to achieve. Calculate how much you anticipate saving and put that figure in the fourth column ("Savings").

Budget Worksheet

EXPENSE	TRACKED MONTH	NEW BUDGET	SAVINGS
HOUSING			
Rent/mortgage			
Home-equity loan			
Heat			
Water			
Electricity			
Insurance			
Phone			
Internet			
Cable			
Lawn/garden			
Repairs			
Other services			
Percent of total (Housing should represent 35 percent.)			
TRANSPORTATION			
Car payment 1			
Car payment 2			
Gasoline			

EXPENSE	TRACKED MONTH	NEW BUDGET	SAVINGS
Insurance			
Repairs/upkeep			
Commuting			
Parking			
Other			
Percent of total (Transportation should represent 15 percent.)			
CREDIT CARDS / LOANS			
Credit card 1			
Credit card 2			
Credit card 3			
Credit card 4			
Other loan 1			
Other loan 2			
Other			
Percent of total (Debt repayment should represent 15 percent.)			
CHILD CARE			
Babysitting			
Tuition			
Clothing			
Lessons			
Toys			
Gifts			
Other			
FOOD			
Groceries			
Eating out			
Entertaining			
Other			

EXPENSE	TRACKED MONTH	NEW BUDGET	SAVINGS
PERSONAL			
Clothing			
Beauty shop/barbershop			
Dry-cleaning			
Health Club			
Cell phone/BlackBerry			
Gifts			
Other			
MEDICAL			
Insurance			
Co-pays			
Prescriptions			
Unreimbursed medical			
ENTERTAINMENT			
Tickets (movies/theater/concert/sports)			
CDs/DVDs			
Books/magazines			
Other			
TRAVEL			
Vacation			
Other			
PETS			
Food			
Medical care			
Grooming			
Other			

EXPENSE	TRACKED MONTH	NEW BUDGET	SAVINGS
OTHER			
Percent of total (All these categories combined should represent 25 percent.)			
SAVINGS/INVESTMENTS			
401(k) contribution			
Other retirement contribution			
Monthly savings			
Percent of total (You're aiming to save 10 percent.)			
Total Anticipated Savings:			

One reason many middle-income families don't save is that they don't believe they can come up with big enough sums of money to do it effectively. The fact is small amounts can be quite effective. Start with a few dollars a day. Then add an automatic transfer from checking to savings every month. Some banks are even willing to transfer money weekly, if moving small amounts more frequently feels easier on your wallet. It sounds trivial but I've heard story after story of people who accumulated hundreds of dollars that way, realized they could do it, and worked harder to get more.

NOTE: If you want to continue to track your spending and saving from month to month, I've included additional worksheets at the back of this journal.

Putting It in Perspective: The Most Important Things in Life Aren't Things

Look back over your tracked month and highlight some of your biggest nonessential purchases (if you haven't spent money on any large items, look for small, repeated expenses on nonessentials). Here are some questions to ask yourself about these purchases:

How did this *object* (iced coffee, new shoes, new flat-screen TV) make me feel?

_____

_____

_____

How long did those feelings last? _____

_____

_____

_____

In contrast, how did some of my *experiences* this month (vacation, cooking class, weekend away, movie) make me feel?

_____

_____

_____

How long did those feelings last? _____

_____

_____

_____

The things that left me most satisfied were: _____

_____

_____

_____

Given this realization, I can cut back my spending on: _____

_____

_____

_____

_____

_____

_____

_____

_____

_____

_____

_____

_____

_____

_____

_____

NOTE: You will likely see what psychologists have noticed: Your money is better spent on experiences rather than things. Experiences get better in the retelling. Things break and tarnish over time. You will also be able to decide more easily where you need and want to spend your money—and where you need to save it.

THE DIFFERENCE
WEALTH-BUILDING JOURNAL

Retirement: How Much Do You Need to Save?

Figuring out how much you need to save—particularly for retirement—seems so complicated that many people don't bother to go through the steps to figure out what their number actually is. That's unfortunate, because if you don't figure out how much you're likely to need, chances are you're not going to save nearly enough. A new study from Hewitt Associates took a look at the projected retirement levels of nearly two million employees at seventy-two large U.S. companies and concluded that fewer than one in five workers will be able to meet 100 percent of their retirement needs. Yikes.

According to the Hewitt study, that's nowhere near enough. They suggest men need to replace 123 percent of their final salaries and women need to replace 130 percent. Those are numbers that may well be out of many people's reach—but shooting for at least 100 percent is smart in my book.

Step 1. Figure out how much you'll get from Social Security.
Go to http://ssa.gov/OACT/quickcalc. Once you're there, select the inflated (future) dollars benefits estimate, not the one that provides the benefit estimate in today's dollars. What you'll see is that delaying Social Security from age sixty-two to age sixty-six can increase your monthly take by a good third. It's a strategy worth considering if you're behind.

Step 2. Fill in this worksheet (or use a retirement calculator on the Web)
Start with the Ballpark E$timate put together by the nonprofit American Savings Education Council (www.choosetosave.org).

If you're not online, you can use this fill-in-the-blank version of the Ballpark E$timate. This worksheet assumes you'll realize a constant real rate of return of 3 percent and that wages will grow at the same rate as inflation; however, it does provide the user an opportunity to take into account longevity risk. If you're married, you and your spouse should each fill out your own worksheet (photocopy this exercise so that you each have your own copy).

The Ballpark E$timate® worksheet was developed by the American Savings Education Council® and the Employee Benefit Research Institute®, and is a registered trademark of EBRI. Further details can be found at www.choosetosave.org. Used with permission.

1. How much annual income will you want in retirement?

Figure at least 70 percent of your current annual gross income just to maintain your current standard of living; however, you may want to enter a larger number. See the tips sidebar.

$_____

2. Subtract the income you expect to receive annually from:

SOCIAL SECURITY. If you make under $25,000, enter $8,000; between $25,000 and $40,000, enter $12,000; over $40,000, enter $14,500. (For married couples, the lower-earning spouse should enter either their own benefit based on their income or 50 percent of the higher-earning spouse's benefit, whichever is higher.)

– $_____

TRADITIONAL EMPLOYER PENSION. A plan that pays a set dollar amount for life, where the dollar amount depends on salary and years of service (in today's dollars).

– $_____

PART-TIME INCOME.

– $_____

OTHER (REVERSE ANNUITY MORTGAGE PAYMENTS, EARNINGS ON ASSETS, ETC.).

– $_____

This is how much you need to make up for each retirement year:

= $_____

Tips to Help You Select an Annual Retirement Income Goal

70 PERCENT TO 80 PERCENT: You will need to pay for the basics in retirement, but you won't have to pay many medical expenses because your employer pays the Medicare premium and provides employer-paid retiree health insurance. You're planning for a comfortable retirement without much travel. You are older and/or in your prime earning years.

80 PERCENT TO 90 PERCENT: You will need to pay your Medicare premiums and pay for insurance to cover medical costs above Medicare, which on average covers about 55 percent. You plan to take some small trips, and you know that you will need to continue saving some money.

100 PERCENT TO 130 PERCENT: You will need to cover all Medicare and other health-care costs. You are very young and/or your prime earning years are ahead of you. You would like a retirement lifestyle that is more than comfortable. You need to save for the possibility of long-term care.

Now you want to estimate how much money you'll need in the bank the day you retire. For the record, we assume you'll realize a constant real rate of return of 3 percent after inflation, and you'll begin to receive income from Social Security at age sixty-five.

3. To determine the amount you'll need to save, multiply the amount you need to make up by the factor below.

AGE YOU EXPECT TO RETIRE	Choose your factor based on life expectancy (at age 65):					
	Male (age 82)	Female (age 86)	Male (age 89)	Female (age 92)	Male (age 94)	Female (age 97)
55	18.79	20.53	21.71	22.79	23.46	24.40
60	16.31	18.32	19.68	20.93	21.71	22.79
65	13.45	15.77	17.35	18.79	19.68	20.93
70	10.15	12.83	14.65	16.31	17.35	18.79

$_____

4. If you expect to retire before age 65, multiply your Social Security benefit from line 2 by the factor below.

Age you expect to retire:
At 55 your factor is 8.8
At 60 your factor is 4.7
+ $_____

5. Multiply your savings to date by the factor below (include money accumulated in a 401(k), IRA, or similar retirement plan).

If you plan to retire in:
10 years your factor is 1.3
15 years your factor is 1.6
20 years your factor is 1.8
25 years your factor is 2.1
30 years your factor is 2.4
35 years your factor is 2.8
40 years your factor is 3.3
– $_____

Total additional savings needed at retirement: = $_____

Don't panic. We devised another formula to show you how much to save each year in order to reach your goal amount. This factors in compounding. That's where your money not only makes interest, your interest starts making interest as well, creating a snowball effect.

6. To determine the *annual* amount you'll need to save, multiply the total amount by the factor below.

If you want to retire in:

10 years your factor is .085

15 years your factor is .052

20 years your factor is .036

25 years your factor is .027

30 years your factor is .020

35 years your factor is .016

40 years your factor is .013

= $_____

It's important to understand that using this or any other calculator is not an exact science; what you're really doing is running scenarios. You can see what happens if you tell the computer you want to work longer, or if your money grows at a faster rate, or if you decide—since your mortgage will be paid off and you don't like to travel anyway—you don't feel you need to (or will never get to) the 123 to 130 percent Hewitt recommends.

What if It's Not Enough?

So many people are behind when it comes to saving for retirement and other big goals that I would not be surprised if you go through this exercise and are blown away. Part of resolving that problem is a matter of saving more. The other part is making some other financial choices.

- **Postpone retirement until sixty-seven.** And don't take Social Security until that time. Putting off your payments increases your monthly take-home by as much as one-third to one-half.
- **Maximize retirement accounts.** Nearly one-third of people didn't contribute to their 401(k) plans in 2007. Of those who did contribute, nearly one-quarter didn't contribute enough to get the employer match. That's leaving free money on the table.

- **Don't withdraw when changing jobs.** Nearly 45 percent of people withdraw money from 401(k)s when they change jobs. This is a savings killer and a huge mistake. It can cost you 20 percent of the balance in federal taxes and 10 percent in early withdrawal penalties.

Coming Up

If one of your goals involves putting aside more money for retirement (extra points for you if it is!) go directly to chapter 2, "Attribute Focus: Investing," to learn more about putting that savings to work.

If one of your financial goals is long term and complex (buying property or starting a business), you will definitely want to proceed to chapter 3, "Attribute Focus: Drive," which is designed to help you break down ambitious goals into manageable pieces.

CHAPTER
№

ATTRIBUTE FOCUS:
INVESTING

Date that I began this chapter: _____/_____/_____

Date that I completed this chapter: _____/_____/_____

INTRODUCTION

It's not enough to earn a decent living—or even a living that is beyond decent. You need to take those earnings and put them to work. Very specifically. In stocks.

In this chapter you'll learn how to work the markets to your advantage while avoiding some of the classic mistakes stock investors tend to make. These exercises are designed to help you find a financial adviser, balance your investment strategy, and calm your nerves if the market is on a roller coaster.

Exercise Checklist
❏ Making Your Money Grow
❏ Finding a Financial Adviser
❏ Tolerating Risk Number One: Acknowledge That You're Scared
❏ Tolerating Risk Number Two: What Happens If I Do This? What Happens If I Don't?

Invest Aggressively but Appropriately

The wealthy buy stocks. To some extent, this entire chapter can be summed up in those four simple words. In our survey, we asked the question in quite a few different ways. But each time the answer was the same: The wealthy buy stocks.

WHICH DESCRIBES THE WAY YOU VIEW THE STOCK MARKET?		
	Too risky for a large portion of my wealth	*Worth the risk of a portion of my wealth because of the returns it can generate*
Wealthy	34 percent	66 percent
Financially comfortable	55 percent	45 percent
Paycheck-to-paychecks	77 percent	23 percent
Further-in-debtors	83 percent	17 percent

Even the question that pointed such a strong finger toward saving was tipped toward sound investing for the wealthy. We asked, "What has been the most important factor in helping you reach your financial status?" For the wealthy, sound investing was the number one answer. Habitual saving was number two.

THE DIFFERENCE
WEALTH-BUILDING JOURNAL

Even the question that pointed such a strong finger toward saving was tipped toward sound investing for the wealthy. We asked, "What has been the most important factor in helping you reach your financial status?" For the wealthy, sound investing was the number one answer. Habitual saving was number two.

Far too many people stop at saving. Others try to dip a toe in the investing waters but make mistakes along the way. Why? The reasons are many, but they tend to revolve around the same thing: risk. Because we are fearful, we don't take the appropriate risks at the appropriate times. So, before I lay out my straightforward and—I believe—relatively simple approach to investing for your future, let's look at the hurdles that may prevent you from implementing this approach effectively.

The Mistakes We Make

WAITING TO BEGIN. There is, was, and always will be another, more pressing, use for your money than putting it away to grow for the future. And because these expenses will all be here much sooner than, say, retirement, they will look much more enticing than a deposit into your 401(k) or IRA. Witness: Investing the same sum of money—let's say $200—month in and month out until you retire at age 65 in a tax-deferred portfolio earning a conservative 8 percent will grow into the following.

If you begin at age 22, at 65 you'll have $901,155.
If you begin at age 32, at 65 you'll have $389,507.
If you begin at age 42, at 65 you'll have $258,998.

NOT DIVERSIFYING. I have to admit, I thought Enron was finally going to do it. I thought all those stories of employees losing their stock-laden nest eggs at the same time they were losing their jobs would convince people that keeping too great a share of their portfolio in one stock—particularly company stock—was a dumb move. And yet, we see it happen every time a major company goes under.

Here's my rule: No more than 10 percent of your assets in any one stock, including company stock. If it's tough to toe that line because you work for a company that provides its 401(k) match in the form of company stock, diversify as soon as possible.

RAIDING A RETIREMENT ACCOUNT. When we leave jobs—which we do an average twelve times over the course of a career—45 percent of us raid our retirement accounts. Why do we do it? Sometimes we forget to roll the money over.

Other times, the balance in the account seems so small and meaningless we are sure it will not amount to a lot over time. We are wrong.

Two thousand dollars invested in a tax-deferred account earning a return of 8 percent will be worth $48,547 forty years down the road.

Five thousand dollars invested in a tax-deferred account earning a return of 8 percent will be worth $54,679 thirty years down the road.

To make matters worse, by pulling the money out, we pay taxes and penalties of 30 percent—sometimes even more. That $2,000 becomes $1,400. That $5,000 becomes $3,500.

TRADING TOO MUCH. According to two recent academic studies, the typical mutual fund turns over 77 percent of its portfolio annually, the average individual investor, 75 percent. And each time we push the button, it eats seriously into our potential profits—not just because we might be buying or selling the wrong things at the wrong times, but because trading in and of itself gets expensive. How to avoid it? Stop trading except when you are rebalancing your portfolio twice a year. And fill your portfolio with index funds (they offer the same diversification as a managed fund, but are less costly to own). Another alternative is to put your money into a target-date retirement fund that will be rebalanced automatically toward your retirement date.

BUYING THE NEXT HOT THING. Our gut tells us to follow a trend, to believe we're on to the next hot hand. The same thing happens to investors. They get on a streak (or more likely, just a bull market) and start believing they are brilliant and can't go wrong. In fact, they can. And it can cost tens of thousands of dollars. The key is to have a plan—a strategy—that determines what and when you buy and what and when you sell (there are exercises for creating exactly this type of plan later in this chapter).

IGNORING UNCLE SAM. Not enough of us max out our 401(k)s. Not enough of us make IRA contributions on a regular basis. Not enough of us kick money into 529 college savings accounts or health savings accounts. We tend to sell winners rather than losers, which results in capital gains taxes. Selling losers, on the other hand, creates tax deductions. We also put the wrong investments—municipal bonds, for example—in tax-advantaged accounts. When you withdraw the money, interests that would otherwise be tax-exempt become fully taxable. The solution lies in getting a hand with some tax planning—you can hire a person for this task or simply buy a tax-software program such as TurboTax. And when you're evaluating mutual funds, pay attention to the after-tax numbers. Morningstar.com often runs after-tax, as well as pre-tax, performance comparisons.

Making Your Money Grow

You need a plan to prevent you from making any and all of these mistakes. You need to set goals, form a strategy, and start viewing the investing of your money as a means to an end—rather than an open-ended process of shoving as much as you can into your 401(k).

Step 1: Take Stock

Figure out how much you need to be putting away monthly to satisfy your retirement goals. Take the annual figure from page 25 in chapter 1, divide by twelve, and write it here: _____

Fill in this chart with information about your current investments to see how your money is allocated now:

TYPE OF ACCOUNT	CURRANT BALANCE/ MARKET VALUE	PERCENT OF TOTAL
Cash (checking, savings, money market)		
Bonds (or CDs, Treasury Bills)		
Stocks		
Mutual funds (or brokerage accounts)		
Employer-sponsored retirement		
Self-directed retirement plan		
TOTAL		

Step 2: Allocate Your Assets

Professional mutual fund managers trying to beat the markets move out of stocks and bonds based on their forecasts of which ones will do particularly well and when. The fact that they have failed so continually has led me and many of the financial experts I respect to the following conclusion: Why even try to beat the market?

Instead of trying to pick stocks or bonds or sectors or funds, buy index funds. They're cheap. They're easy. And you can cover your bases with a money market fund and three index funds (to find a good one with low fees, go to www.morningstar.com):

- A total stock market index fund (domestic)
- A total bond market index fund
- An international stock market index fund

How do you decide how much to put in each kind of fund? It depends on your age (and how close you are to retirement) and your risk tolerance—and the former should largely determine the latter.

TWENTIES TO THIRTIES: EARLY CAREER

50 percent total stock market index fund
20 percent international stock market index fund
20 percent total bond market index fund
10 percent cash or money market fund

FORTIES TO FIFTIES: MIDCAREER

45 percent total stock market index fund
15 percent international stock market index fund
30 percent total bond market index fund
10 percent cash or money market fund

SIXTIES TO SEVENTIES: LATE CAREER, EARLY RETIREMENT

35 percent total stock market index fund
10 percent international stock market index fund
40 percent total bond market index fund
15 percent cash or money market fund

EIGHTIES AND OLDER: RETIREMENT

25 percent total stock market index fund
 5 percent international stock market index fund
40 percent total bond market index fund
30 percent cash or money market fund

Step 3: Rebalance Your Accounts

The only thing required if you go this route is maintenance. Twice a year—on your birthday, let's say, or right around Christmas and the fourth of July—you need to take a look at your accounts. If stocks have gone on a tear, you may need to sell some of your stock fund and buy some shares of your bond fund to right your asset allocations. If bonds have had a tremendous run, you may need to sell some shares of your bond fund and buy some of your stock fund to do the same. When you make major changes to the balance of investments, make note of your reason for doing so.

REBALANCING NOTES				
Date	**Percent in Stocks**	**Percent in Bonds**	**Percent in Cash**	**Percent Other**

Reason for Rebalance:

Reason for Rebalance:

Reason for Rebalance:

Reason for Rebalance:

Reason for Rebalance:

Reason for Rebalance:

Reason for Rebalance:

Reason for Rebalance:

Reason for Rebalance:

Reason for Rebalance:

REBALANCING NOTES

Date	Percent in Stocks	Percent in Bonds	Percent in Cash	Percent Other

Reason for Rebalance:

Reason for Rebalance:

Reason for Rebalance:

Reason for Rebalance:

Reason for Rebalance:

Reason for Rebalance:

Reason for Rebalance:

Reason for Rebalance:

Reason for Rebalance:

Reason for Rebalance:

REBALANCING NOTES				
Date	**Percent in Stocks**	**Percent in Bonds**	**Percent in Cash**	**Percent Other**

Reason for Rebalance:

Reason for Rebalance:

Reason for Rebalance:

Reason for Rebalance:

Reason for Rebalance:

Reason for Rebalance:

Reason for Rebalance:

Reason for Rebalance:

Reason for Rebalance:

Reason for Rebalance:

Finding a Financial Adviser

If you are concerned about balancing your portfolio and making investment decisions on your own, here's how to go about finding a good financial adviser.

Step 1. Generate a short list of names.

Ask colleagues (who are likely in a similar financial situation or at least in the same industry) for recommendations. What if you can't gather enough recommendations to create a short list? The following are websites of prominent financial planning organizations. Each has a locator service.

- **Fpanet.org:** The website of the Financial Planning Association, the largest membership of financial advisers.
- **NAPFA.org:** The website of the National Association of Personal Financial Advisors, an organization for fee-only financial advisers.
- **Garrettplanningnetwork.com:** A website of the Garrett Planning Network, which is made up of fee-only financial advisers, many of whom are willing to work by the hour.

POSSIBLE ADVISERS:

_____

_____

_____

_____

Step 2. Set up interviews and ask the following questions.

Copy this interview if you want to take notes on several different candidates.

NAME/COMPANY: _____

HOW WILL YOU BE PAID? _____

_____

_____

_____

HOW MUCH WILL THIS RELATIONSHIP COST ME OVER ONE YEAR?

_____

HOW WILL YOU EVALUATE MY RISK LEVEL? WHAT LEVEL OF RISK DO YOU RECOMMEND FOR ME?

_____

_____

_____

_____

ASK FOR REFERENCES AND FOLLOW UP (YOU CAN ASK TO SEE A PLAN THAT THIS ADVISER HAS PREPARED FOR SOMEONE ELSE—WITH NO NAMES OR IDENTIFYING DETAILS, OF COURSE).

REFERENCES:

_____

_____

_____

_____

_____

Step 3. Make a gut call.

Is this someone you feel comfortable talking to about money? Is this someone you'd be comfortable disclosing past financial mistakes to? It is imperative that you're able to have an open and honest conversation with whomever you hire.

_____

_____

_____

_____

_____

_____

Tolerating Risk Number One: Acknowledge That You're Scared

One of the most important things to know as you approach any risk—financial or otherwise—is that it is normal to be anxious. When you read in the newspaper or see some analyst on TV shouting about how the housing market is crashing or that your stocks are worthless, acknowledge that you are scared and put your concerns down on paper. Then ask yourself, "How realistic are these fears?" Follow my example:

What are your fears?

I'm afraid that I probably bought my home at the top of the market. If I had to sell today, I'd be out six figures.

_____

_____

_____

_____

_____

_____

_____

How realistic are these fears?

No loss is real until you have to take it, and I'm not planning to move for several years.

_____

_____

_____

_____

_____

_____

_____

Tolerating Risk Number Two: What Happens If I Do This? What Happens If I Don't?

The risk of inaction should always be pondered, yet all too often it's forgotten. When you approach any risk, ask yourself these questions:

What happens to me if I do this?

_____

_____

_____

_____

_____

_____

What happens to me if I don't do this?

_____

_____

_____

_____

_____

_____

What choice does my gut tell me to make?

_____

_____

_____

_____

_____

_____

Start thinking long term. This is the strategy that drives the most successful investors. It is not about today, tomorrow, next month, or even next year. It is about the next decade and the decade after that. This is the window through which you should process all questions about your money: Where do I want to be one year from now, ten years from now, thirty years from now? Does making this investment move me closer or further away?

Coming Up

When it comes to saving and investing, this much is clear: You'll be able to make the right decisions in the moment—and correct your path along the way—if you are fully in touch with your life goals. And that is precisely what the next chapter of this journal is about.

CHAPTER
№
3

ATTRIBUTE FOCUS:
DRIVE

Date that I began this chapter: _____/_____/_____

Date that I completed this chapter: _____/_____/_____

INTRODUCTION

In chapter 1, you charted your spending habits and created a new budget that will allow you to save and invest more aggressively. The point of this chapter is to help you set and reach these goals and make The Difference a part of your life.

You'll remember in chapter 1, "Attribute Focus: Saving," that one of the biggest obstacles to achieving long-term goals is that our brains are hard-wired for short-term gratification. The exercises in this chapter are designed to help you set concrete goals, break them down in manageable pieces, and deal with the fact that reaching them in the long term almost always means over-coming some short-term obstacles. These principals aren't restricted to making financial gains; they'll help you stick to any new program and achieve any goal you set for yourself. It's time to turn complicated goals into realities.

Exercise Checklist
❑ Hedonic Calculus
❑ What Makes a Goal Achievable?
❑ Some Goals Are Better Than Others
❑ Mapping Your Goal
❑ Stick-with-It Strategy Number One: Visualize Your Goals
❑ Stick-with-It Strategy Number Two: Tell Someone

Ambition: The Wanting Is Paramount
You've got the desire. You've got the ambition. How do you get yourself to make a commitment to—and then stick with—the tenets of The Difference? Icek Aizen, a psychology professor at the University of Massachusetts, has studied precisely that: the psychology of action. How do you get yourself to do something that you want to do?

It seems to be a no-brainer of a question. But, as Aizen explains, even goals that seem on the surface to be 100 percent positive have negative elements embedded. The long-term benefits you reap are at war with the short-term compromises you have to make.

Consider a goal of saving more money. You can believe with your entire being that saving money is a good thing in the long term. But in the immediate future, the fact that you're putting away your money rather than spending it has not-so-desirable consequences. It may mean you can't eat out as often. Or that you have to wash the car yourself. The fact that the positives—putting your kids through college with a minimum of loans, or a lush retirement—come years down the road doesn't help matters.

Goals also require that you sacrifice time. Many—retirement, raising children, attaining happiness that's lasting rather than fleeting, growing wealth—are not one-time events. You can't simply check these things off your list. Rather, they will take years. They may take decades. And in the meantime, you'll have all sorts of other goals you want to pursue.

Distinguish Goals from Fantasies

We all have fantasies in our lives. They're things that we want and often express to others. ("I want to change jobs." "I want a second child." "I want to save more money." "I want to be happier." "I want to retire.") Fantasies all, and fantasies they will remain until we break them down and figure out (a) what is standing between the place we are now and the place where we have acquired or accomplished those things, and (b) if we are willing to make the sacrifices necessary to get there.

The fact that you want many things simultaneously makes it difficult to allow one to float to the top. It is easier to decide what the most important goal for the short term is and use your willpower to accomplish it without allowing yourself to get sidetracked. It's much harder to set priorities when you're dealing in a time frame longer than a few days, but that's precisely what you have to do. You have to decide whether it's more important to you to go on that one-time vacation or to put away $2,000. These are questions that can be tough to answer. The next few exercises will help.

Hedonic Calculus

It is very likely that you have many competing goals in your life. How can you satisfy them all? Or at least prevent the quest for one goal from sabotaging your chances of achieving the others? You do it by performing what the psychological community calls a "hedonic calculus."

First, without editing yourself, make a list of everything that you want to accomplish (financially and otherwise) below. Next, go through this list and rank these goals. Which are crucial? Which can wait? Which, in the scheme of things, don't matter much at all? Do you keep postponing the real goal until it never becomes a reality?

Goal	Rank

Date: ____/____/____

What Makes a Goal Achievable?

How do you know when your goals are right for you? How do you know when they're actually achievable? For your goal—whether it's one you've set for yourself or one someone else has set for you—to be one that you can realize, it has to have four distinct qualities.

Choose the most important financial goal from your hedonic calculus, and rephrase it in one complete sentence: *I want to*

_____

_____

Now answer the following key questions:

1. The Buy-In: Goals don't work unless you're ready. You have to want it. Why do you want to achieve this goal?

_____

_____

_____

_____

2. Achievability: If you want to run a marathon, you won't cross that finish line if you don't believe you have the stuff. You're better off going for a half-marathon or 10K first. Likewise, you can't meet a goal unless you define its specific parameters. For example, your goal may be "I want to be successful in my career." Does that mean getting a promotion in eighteen months, or earning tacit approval from your supervisor that you're doing a good job? Is your goal stated specifically enough, and do you believe that you can achieve it?

_____

_____

_____

_____

_____

_____

3. Positive Impact: A goal is more achievable—and researchers have found you'll be more committed to it—if its overall impact on your life will be positive. How will you feel when you reach this goal? What impact will reaching it have on your life?

_____

_____

_____

_____

_____

4. Complexity: A powerful, far-reaching goal will have several hurdles to overcome and benchmarks to reach (you'll explore those in more detail later). If reaching a goal is too easy, then in your mind you don't accomplish anything by getting there. For example, "opening a savings account" would be one benchmark in a larger goal, not the end goal itself. Does your goal require multiple steps?

_____

_____

_____

_____

_____

_____

_____

_____

_____

Some Goals Are Better Than Others

The headline above sounds like a value judgment. It's not. The thing that makes some goals better than others is not the what, but the why. If your goal is wealth—money, riches, cold hard cash—the parameters are exactly the same. The primary issue is not whether you want wealth. The primary issue is *why* you want it. People who focus outside of themselves, setting goals that are more constructive and collaborative, often feel calm, connected, and clear. These positive emotions help keep the most important goals at the forefront and encourage getting things done rather than procrastinating.

Put your goal to the test again. What is your motive for wanting to create wealth? Who—aside from you—will benefit if you reach your goal?

_____

_____

_____

_____

_____

_____

_____

_____

_____

_____

_____

_____

_____

_____

_____

_____

Mapping Your Goals

Once you have a goal that seems to have the four key characteristics (buy-in, achievability, positive impact, and complexity), then it's time to chunk it out. Think about your goal as if it were a set of MapQuest directions. Each time you're supposed to make a left or a right turn, or merge onto the parkway, you pause, you think, you act. Those are benchmarks.

Now, take your top financial goal and break it down into smaller, more manageable pieces, and map your way to success. Seeing your goals formed into actual words helps emphasize their seriousness; it makes them feel more real.

The Goal: _____

_____

_____

Total Anticipated Time Commitment: _____

Expectations and Hurdles: What do you expect will get in your way of achieving this goal? What sacrifices do you expect you will have to make?

_____

_____

_____

_____

_____

Benchmarks: This is where you map out the individual steps you need to take to achieve your goal. Break down each benchmark into time commit ments and smaller hurdles. Once you embark on this plan, take notes on your progress.

Benchmark Number 1: _____

ANTICIPATED TIME COMMITMENT TO REACH THIS BENCHMARK: _____

_____

EXPECTATIONS (HOW WILL I REACH THIS BENCHMARK?): _____

_____

_____

HURDLES (SACRIFICES AND CHALLENGES I MAY ENCOUNTER AS I REACH FOR THIS BENCHMARK):

_____

_____

CHECK-IN / PROGRESS NOTES: _____

_____

_____

Benchmark Number 2: _____

ANTICIPATED TIME COMMITMENT TO REACH THIS BENCHMARK: _____

_____

EXPECTATIONS (HOW WILL I REACH THIS BENCHMARK?): _____

_____

_____

HURDLES (SACRIFICES AND CHALLENGES I MAY ENCOUNTER AS I REACH FOR THIS BENCHMARK):

_____

_____

CHECK-IN / PROGRESS NOTES: _____

_____

_____

Benchmark Number 3: _____

ANTICIPATED TIME COMMITMENT TO REACH THIS BENCHMARK: _____

_____

_____

EXPECTATIONS (HOW WILL I REACH THIS BENCHMARK?): _____

_____

_____

HURDLES (SACRIFICES AND CHALLENGES I MAY ENCOUNTER AS I REACH FOR THIS BENCHMARK):

_____

_____

CHECK-IN / PROGRESS NOTES: _____

_____

Benchmark Number 4: _____

ANTICIPATED TIME COMMITMENT TO REACH THIS BENCHMARK: _____

_____

EXPECTATIONS (HOW WILL I REACH THIS BENCHMARK?): _____

_____

_____

HURDLES (SACRIFICES AND CHALLENGES I MAY ENCOUNTER AS I REACH FOR THIS BENCHMARK):

_____

_____

CHECK-IN / PROGRESS NOTES: _____

_____

_____

Benchmark Number 5: _____

ANTICIPATED TIME COMMITMENT TO REACH THIS BENCHMARK: _____

_____

_____

EXPECTATIONS (HOW WILL I REACH THIS BENCHMARK?): _____

_____

_____

HURDLES (SACRIFICES AND CHALLENGES I MAY ENCOUNTER AS I REACH FOR THIS BENCHMARK):

_____

_____

CHECK-IN / PROGRESS NOTES: _____

_____

_____

Benchmark Number 6: _____

ANTICIPATED TIME COMMITMENT TO REACH THIS BENCHMARK: _____

_____

EXPECTATIONS (HOW WILL I REACH THIS BENCHMARK?): _____

_____

_____

HURDLES (SACRIFICES AND CHALLENGES I MAY ENCOUNTER AS I REACH FOR THIS BENCHMARK):

_____

_____

CHECK-IN / PROGRESS NOTES: _____

_____

_____

_____

NOTE: As you put your plan into action, you may need to make revisions if unanticipated opportunities or hurdles come your way. People often see initial success or partial progress as an excuse to disengage from their goals. Similarly, they see initial resistance as an excuse to get out before "wasting" any additional effort. The key is knowing how long it will likely take you to get

Stick-with-It Strategy: Visualize Your Goals

There will be a time as you're reaching for any benchmark or goal that you will feel your resolve beginning to slip. Chances are, you are experiencing either the "What the Hell?" Effect or the "I Deserve It" Effect. The "What the Hell?" Effect usually happens early in the process; you feel a little discouraged by your tiny accumulation of savings and think, "What the hell, I might as well just spend it." The "I Deserve It" Effect usually happens after you've been saving for a while; you feel great about your progress and decide to treat yourself on a whim.

The key to combating these moments is to make your goal as concrete as you can. You need to be able not only to describe it, but to see it. If your goal is buying your dream house, find a home that you admire and take a snapshot of it. Then make it your screensaver and put it on your fridge. And while you're at it, attach a date to that dream, so that in your mind you're not only living in that four-bedroom Cotswold, you're living in that four-bedroom Cotswold on July 23, 2013.

Take a moment to fill the next two pages with your most vivid visualization of your goal (include dates and specific details). If you want, attach a picture.

_____

_____

_____

_____

_____

_____

_____

_____

_____

_____

_____

Stick-with-It Strategy: Tell Someone

Find a friend, a spouse, or someone else to be a cheerleader to help you overcome your natural urges and get you to your goal. If you're feeling your resistance start to wane, this person will become the go-to guy or gal whose job it is to talk you out of it.

Think about who in your life would be an excellent cheerleader. Tell this person about your goal and get him/her to sign this pledge:

It is my duty to remind _____ of his/her goal to
_____. As his/her official cheerleader,
I will do everything in my power to encourage saving and discourage frivolous spending.

Signed: _____ **Dated:** _____

NOTE: You can now do this on the Internet. Yale professors Dean Karlan and Ian Ayres just launched a website called StickK.com that allows you to post your goal, notify your friends, and then set up a series of penalties if you fail to come through.

Coming Up

We've established that living The Difference is a choice. For some people, it's deeper than that. It's a drive that's innate—fueled by competitive juices that spur you to work hard and get ahead. The definition of hard work is not what it used to be, however. Sure, putting in the hours is often part of the process—but making the most of those hours is even more important. Are you ready to find out how to get your hard work to work for you? Coming right up in chapter 4 . . .

CHAPTER
№
4

ATTRIBUTE FOCUS:
HARD WORK

Date that I began this chapter: _____/_____/_____

Date that I completed this chapter: _____/_____/_____

INTRODUCTION

Over the past few years, the country has been taken with the notion that working smart, working ultra-efficiently, is far better than working hard—when, in fact, both smart work and hard work are needed to make The Difference.

In this chapter, you'll learn about grit—and whether you have it. You'll see how your tendencies to put in the hours (or not) measures up to the population around you. This series of exercises will teach you how to find the gumption to dig into a particular project even when you don't quite "feel it" in your soul, and why—at particular points in your life—working hard is absolutely necessary to build wealth. As you complete each exercise, check it off the list below.

Exercise Checklist
❑ How Conscientious Are You?
❑ Competition Brings Out Our Best
❑ Toot Your Own Horn
❑ Evaluate Three Workdays
❑ Rebalance Your Priorities
❑ Time Is Money

Working Hard *and* Working Smart
Let's talk about what it means to work hard. Does it mean you put in the hours—more, say, than the guy or gal at the next desk? Does it mean working until the work is done? Or getting more done in the same amount of time? Yes. To all of the above. And it is necessary for success and necessary for wealth, especially in recent years when job security has been limited.

DOES THE WORD "HARDWORKING" DESCRIBE YOU VERY WELL?	PERCENT THAT ANSWERED "YES"
Wealthy	72 percent
Financially comfortable	62 percent
Paycheck-to-paychecks	68 percent
Further-in-debtors	67 percent

These are notably slimmer differences than we saw for other measures such as optimism and resilience. But, notes Duke University finance scholar David Robinson, that is likely because our survey takers may have been uncomfortable admitting that they do not work hard, no matter what category they fall into.

It is obvious in any working environment that some people are, in fact, more hardworking than others. Why is it that some teens are willing to scoop double chocolate chip on a Saturday night when others aren't, or that some executives put the kids to bed then put in a second shift at the computer, rather than let the company down? Where does that drive come from?

It's Called Grit

Back in the years after World War II, psychologists started to wonder if there was a way to organize the almost infinite number of ways that human beings differ from one another. By the late 1960s and early '70s the researchers had determined that all personality traits, in fact, could be lumped together by their similarities into five larger personality buckets: extroversion, agreeableness, conscientiousness, emotional stability, and intellect.

Working hard falls into the conscientiousness bucket.

Conscientiousness encompasses traits including being punctual, ambitious, and orderly, as well as two factors that deserve elaboration: competitiveness and something that University of Pennsylvania psychologist Angela Duckworth calls "grit." When you have grit you are a hard worker. You have stamina and are able to persevere to achieve your long-term goals. You are focused, dedicated, self-controlled, and finish what you start, even when you're down. Which, of course, leads to succeeding financially.

This chapter will provide you with strategies for channeling your time and effort into the areas of your work and personal life that matter the most. If you are going to put in the hours, you'll want to make sure that your effort is paying off (both financially and personally). That's what The Difference is really all about.

How Conscientious Are You?

Here are a number of characteristics that may or may not apply to you. For example, do you agree that—as it says in question 1—you are always prepared? Write a number next to each statement that indicates the extent to which you agree or disagree with that statement based on the following scale:

1 = **Disagree strongly**
2 = **Disagree a little**
3 = **Neither agree nor disagree**
4 = **Agree a little**
5 = **Agree strongly**

1. Am always prepared.	
2. Pay attention to details.	
3. Make a mess of things.	
4. Get chores done right away.	
5. Leave my belongings around.	
6. Often forget to put things back in their proper places.	
7. Shirk my duties.	
8. Follow a schedule.	
9. Like order.	
10. Neglect my duties.	
11. Am exacting in my work.	
12. Waste my time.	
13. Do things according to a plan.	
14. Continue until everything is perfect.	
15. Make plans and stick to them.	
16. Do things in a halfway manner.	
17. Find it difficult to get down to work.	
18. Leave a mess in my room.	
19. Love order and regularity.	
20. Like to tidy up.	

TO SCORE: For questions 1, 2, 4, 8, 9, 11, 13, 14, 15, 19, and 20, simply add up the numbers. Score questions 3, 5, 6, 7, 10, 12, 16, 17, and 18 in reverse. (5 = 1; 4 = 2; 3 = 3; 2 = 4; 5 = 1). Then add up your numbers. The higher your score, the more hardworking you are.

INTERPRETING YOUR SCORE: Just like answering direct questions about whether you are hardworking brings out a bias in respondents (we don't like to acknowledge it if we are not working hard), many of these items do as well.

The highest possible score is 100.

At 85 or above, you are very conscientious.

At 70 to 85, you are about average.

Below 70, there's ample room for improvement.

EXERCISE

Date: ___/___/___

Competition Brings Out Our Best

Studies have shown that most people perform better when they have something or someone to beat. Try competing against yourself, first. What is your personal best?

Think about one area of your performance that can be measured (meeting deadlines, writing excellent copy, or staying on budget) and ask yourself how you can take it to the next level (beating a deadline, writing copy with fewer requests for revisions, coming in under budget).

_____

_____

_____

_____

_____

_____

_____

_____

Toot Your Own Horn

There are times you engage in competition—often on the job—when those who have your paycheck and review in their hands might not realize it. That's when you need to toot your own horn. You need to be able to explain your own output in the supervisor's language. You're not bragging. You're explaining the value you bring to the organization.

That means tracking your own production, taking good notes on what you accomplish, and using those notes to inform your next performance review. Start making a list here:

_____

_____

_____

_____

_____

_____

_____

_____

_____

_____

_____

_____

_____

_____

_____

_____

_____

_____

_____

EXERCISE | Date: ___/___/___

Time Is Money

How else can you determine if you are spending your time wisely? It helps to know how much your time is worth. Here's a quick and dirty formula:

Say you make $50,000 a year. Remove the last three zeros. Divide the number in half and you get your approximate hourly rate. In this case, $25. If you make $100,000 a year do the same thing. Lop off the zeros ($100), divide in half, and you get $50.

YOUR ANNUAL INCOME _____

REMOVE THE LAST THREE ZEROS _____

DIVIDE THIS NUMBER BY TWO

(THIS IS WHAT YOUR TIME IS WORTH IN DOLLARS PER HOUR) =_____

There is a point at which putting in the hours becomes little more than banging your head against the wall. For most people, that barrier hits when you are putting in about fifty hours per week. You begin to show signs of wear and tear. Your temper shortens. Your stress level rises. What do you do then? Stop and answer these questions: What work activities are consuming more of my life than I actually think they are? Am I spending hours and hours unconsciously doing things that are not worth my time?

EXERCISE

Evaluate Three Workdays

This is an important time-management study—instead of tracking how you spend money, you are going to track how you spend that other precious commodity—time.

For three days, keep a log of how you spend your workday, using the worksheet on the next page. Every hour, pause to write down what you were doing, breaking that hour into thirty-minute increments.

At the end of the day, go back over your log and give each thirty-minute increment two ratings on a scale of 1 (lowest) to 5 (highest): the first for the satisfaction you took from the time (in the "S" column), the second for whether the activity was productive—generating a reward for you or your company (in the "P" column).

WORKDAY 1   Date: _____/_____/_____

HOURS	TASK	"S" RATING	"P" RATING
7:00–7:30 a.m.			
7:30–8:00 a.m.			
8:00–8:30 a.m.			
8:30–9:00 a.m.			
9:00–9:30 a.m.			
9:30–10:00 a.m.			
10:00–10:30 a.m.			
10:30–11:00 a.m.			
11:00–11:30 a.m.			
11:30–12:00 p.m.			
12:00–12:30 p.m.			
12:30–1:00 p.m.			
1:00–1:30 p.m.			
1:30–2:00 p.m.			
2:00–2:30 p.m.			
2:30–3:00 p.m.			
3:00–3:30 p.m.			
3:30–4:00 p.m.			
4:00–4:30 p.m.			
4:30–5:00 p.m.			
5:00–5:30 p.m.			
5:30–6:00 p.m.			
6:00–6:30 p.m.			
6:30–7:00 p.m.			
Extra Hours			

WORKDAY 2   Date: _____ / _____ / _____

HOURS	TASK	"S" RATING	"P" RATING
7:00–7:30 a.m.			
7:30–8:00 a.m.			
8:00–8:30 a.m.			
8:30–9:00 a.m.			
9:00–9:30 a.m.			
9:30–10:00 a.m.			
10:00–10:30 a.m.			
10:30–11:00 a.m.			
11:00–11:30 a.m.			
11:30–12:00 p.m.			
12:00–12:30 p.m.			
12:30–1:00 p.m.			
1:00–1:30 p.m.			
1:30–2:00 p.m.			
2:00–2:30 p.m.			
2:30–3:00 p.m.			
3:00–3:30 p.m.			
3:30–4:00 p.m.			
4:00–4:30 p.m.			
4:30–5:00 p.m.			
5:00–5:30 p.m.			
5:30–6:00 p.m.			
6:00–6:30 p.m.			
6:30–7:00 p.m.			
Extra Hours			

WORKDAY 3 Date: _____/_____/_____

HOURS	TASK	"S" RATING	"P" RATING
7:00–7:30 a.m.			
7:30–8:00 a.m.			
8:00–8:30 a.m.			
8:30–9:00 a.m.			
9:00–9:30 a.m.			
9:30–10:00 a.m.			
10:00–10:30 a.m.			
10:30–11:00 a.m.			
11:00–11:30 a.m.			
11:30–12:00 p.m.			
12:00–12:30 p.m.			
12:30–1:00 p.m.			
1:00–1:30 p.m.			
1:30–2:00 p.m.			
2:00–2:30 p.m.			
2:30–3:00 p.m.			
3:00–3:30 p.m.			
3:30–4:00 p.m.			
4:00–4:30 p.m.			
4:30–5:00 p.m.			
5:00–5:30 p.m.			
5:30–6:00 p.m.			
6:00–6:30 p.m.			
6:30–7:00 p.m.			
Extra Hours			

Evaluation of the Three Days

After three days, go back and run a quick calculation of what percentage of your days were (a) satisfying, and (b) productive. What percentage of your days ranked 3 or above? (We're aiming for 80 percent.)

DAY 1

Satisfaction Rating

How many thirty-minute segments ranked 3 or above? ____ (Total hours: ____)
How many thirty-minute segments ranked 2 or below?____ (Total hours: ____)
Total up your hours for the day. What percentage of those hours was satisfying?: _____ %

Productivity Rating

How many thirty-minute segments ranked 3 or above? ____ (Total hours: ____)
How many thirty-minute segments ranked 2 or below?____ (Total hours: ____)
Total up your hours for the day. What percentage of those hours was productive?: _____%

DAY 2

Satisfaction Rating

How many thirty-minute segments ranked 3 or above? ____ (Total hours: ____)
How many thirty-minute segments ranked 2 or below?____ (Total hours: ____)
What percentage of your day was satisfying?: _____ %

Productivity Rating

How many thirty-minute segments ranked 3 or above? ____ (Total hours: ____)
How many thirty-minute segments ranked 2 or below?____ (Total hours: ____)
What percentage of your day was productive?: _____ %

DAY 3

Satisfaction Rating

How many thirty-minute segments ranked 3 or above? ____ (Total hours: ____)
How many thirty-minute segments ranked 2 or below?____ (Total hours: ____)
What percentage of your day was productive?: _____ %

Productivity Rating

How many thirty-minute segments ranked 3 or above? ____ (Total hours: ____)
How many thirty-minute segments ranked 2 or below?____ (Total hours: ____)
What percentage of your day was productive?: _____ %

Rebalance Your Priorities

In both satisfaction and productivity, 80 percent of your day should rate at least a 3 or above (and you are aiming for as many 4s and 5s as possible). Over the next week, try to schedule yourself so that more of your time is spent on satisfying and productive activities. Put these items at the top of your to-do list. Talk to your supervisor about taking on more of these kinds of responsibility.

Delegate the things you ranked a 1 or 2, or if you are unable to delegate, allot yourself one or two hours at the end of each day and tell yourself you'll have that time period to get those activities done. Eventually, you'll find you're spending more of your time doing the things you find satisfying and productive. The people you work for and with will notice the improvement as well.

A list of activities that I find highly satisfying and/or productive (ranked 3 or above):

_____

_____

_____

_____

_____

_____

_____

_____

_____

_____

_____

_____

_____

_____

_____

_____

_____

A list of activities that I find unsatisfying and/or unproductive (ranked 2 or lower):

_____

_____

_____

_____

_____

_____

_____

_____

_____

_____

_____

_____

_____

_____

_____

_____

Coming Up

According to my research, the wealthy work harder—and sleep less—than other people. They are more likely to mix work with their downtime as well, sacrificing personal time for professional success. But, because they tend to be passionate about what they do, they are less likely to see work as a chore.

Remember when you were six years old and wanted to be a veterinarian? Or a pilot? Or a teacher? It was a vision that filled you with passion and joy. Unfortunately, as we age we lose that childlike excitement for life's projects. People who understand The Difference get it back. Move on to chapter 5 to discover how harnessing your passion will help sustain you on your journey to wealth.

CHAPTER
№

ATTRIBUTE FOCUS:

PASSION AND CURIOSITY

Date that I began this chapter: _____/_____/_____

Date that I completed this chapter: _____/_____/_____

The more passionate you are about your work, the more likely you are to find something you love and stick with it, and the more likely you are to get wealthy doing it.

In this chapter you'll figure out how to find your passion (or, in the interim, how to get a little more hot and bothered about what you're doing now) and how to translate it into financial success. If you're curious about a subject, I suggest that you find ways to pursue this spark of interest. The wealthy all demonstrate a continuous ability to learn—and not necessarily in a classroom.

Exercise Checklist

PLAN A: PURSUE YOUR PASSION

- ❏ Ten Questions to Pinpoint Your Passion
- ❏ Build a Passion
- ❏ Turn a Passion into a Goal
- ❏ Before You Quit Your Day Job

PLAN B: BRING MORE PASSION TO YOUR CURRENT WORK

- ❏ Forge a Personal Connection with Your Boss
- ❏ Find the Autonomy in Your Job
- ❏ Change Jobs, Not Careers
- ❏ Visualize the Next Logical Step

Job, Career, or Calling?

Follow your bliss. Find your passion. Do what you love.

We have, every single one of us, heard those words. And we are, clearly, trying. At least if trying is something you can measure in hours on the clock. Data from the 2008 study of the National Sleep Foundation shows the average worker spends nine and a half hours at the workplace each day topped off by another four and a half hours working from home. That's a fourteen-hour workday. But research from the conference board shows that only 50 percent of people are satisfied with their jobs today. That's down from 79 percent in 1985, which represents a huge slide in the past 20 years.

On the other hand, the wealthy, and to some degree, the financially comfortable, tell a different story. They are far more likely to like what they do and significantly more likely to say they are "passionate" about it.

I AM PASSIONATE ABOUT MY WORK	PERCENT THAT AGREED
Wealthy	44 percent
Financially comfortable	39 percent
Paycheck-to-paychecks	33 percent
Further-in-Debtors	33 percent

Perhaps this is because they've always had some sense of what line of work would fit them best. They were far less likely to be the ones in college switching from major to major until they ended up on the five- or six-year plan struggling to find the right path.

"I HAVE ALWAYS KNOWN WHAT I WANTED TO DO FOR A CAREER."	PERCENT THAT AGREED
Wealthy	32 percent
Financially comfortable	22 percent
Paycheck-to-paychecks	16 percent
Further-in-debtors	14 percent

In a nutshell, here's what we know: People who are passionate about what they do reach financial comfort and wealth more often than those who are not. That argues for doing one of two things: finding your passion and pursuing it, or becoming passionate about what you're pursuing already. This chapter includes exercises for doing both. Think of establishing yourself in a career that is completely aligned with your passion as "Plan A." At the same time, think about infusing more passion into your current job—and reaping the rewards of doing so—as "Plan B."

Plan B Funds Plan A

There are two important lessons to take from this chapter. The first is that every person has a passion (or three) waiting to be unlocked. The second is that you simply can't afford to wait to start working—and working hard—until you find it. While you are test-driving various ideas and opportunities, you need to have some sort of career or profession or job with potential for growth where, even though you have certain reservations about it, you go ahead and do it. You can't know what you'll unleash until you go for it wholeheartedly.

This entails organizing your life in terms of a Plan B that goes beyond this month, even this year. It means recognizing that working in a job or succeeding in a career that's not the be-all and end-all for you but provides you with stability, benefits, and—yes—money to go home at the end of the day to enjoy your family and pursue nonwork passions. It also provides you with something more important: financing. If and when you find the true thing that you want to do, you'll probably have much more in terms of resources to do it. That argument should be part of the motivating, internal conversation you have with yourself. "I'm going to use Plan B to fund Plan A, once I figure out exactly what Plan A is going to be."

Plan A: Pursue Your Passion

Asking yourself the following questions can help you focus on your passion and understand what it is telling you about your career path. Try to be as honest as possible with your answers. You're not roped into changing your life based on what you say or feel here, but unless you allow yourself to go deep, you're missing the point. If you're going to move toward these desires, they have to come out.

Ten Questions to Pinpoint Your Passion

1. If money was *not* an issue, what would you be doing with your life?

_____

_____

2. When you go to the magazine racks or the library, what do you most like to read about? (Alternately, what do you find yourself searching for on the Internet?)

_____

_____

3. Think about the last few times you said to yourself, "I'd like to do that sometime." What was "that"?

_____

_____

4. What do other people say you do particularly well?

_____

_____

_____

5. Think back to how you felt when you were ten or twelve and try to remember how it felt to be really excited about the possibility of doing something. What could you do today that might make you feel the same way?

_____

_____

_____

6. What do you secretly dream about doing?

_____

_____

7. What are the things you like about what you're doing now? (They can be small, but you have to name several of them.)

_____

_____

8. What do you think you do particularly well? (These things do not have to be work related.)

_____

_____

_____

9. How do you feel you contribute or could contribute to society?

_____

_____

_____

10. What do you want your children (or friends) to say about you when you're gone?

_____

_____

_____

NOTE: As you answer the questions, you'll start to see patterns. They may reflect hidden desires or things that you've perhaps buried—that you wanted in the past and haven't thought about for quite some time. Or they may reflect desires you are aware of but have not—for a wide number of reasons, from financial to emotional—pursued.

Build a Passion

Sure, some people are born knowing they have to be doctors or landscape artists or architects. Others are not, but you can—if you have a sliver of interest in something—turn it into a passion. How? By learning more about it, then practicing it (if, like cooking or karate, it is something that can be practiced). Something that scares you or makes you nervous is actually a signal that you may be on the right track. If not knowing how to do something has you feeling like an idiot, it's an indication that you care about doing it better.

Jot down some hobbies or skills you'd like to pursue by taking a class, joining a group, practicing on your own, or entering a competition.

_____

_____

_____

_____

Once you've started, come back to this page and write about your experience. Was it fun to learn? Intimidating? Is your passion building or dwindling? Did you discover something about yourself you didn't know before?

_____

_____

_____

_____

_____

Turn a Passion into a Goal

Passions are similar to goals. If your answers to the ten questions all pointed to a specific career pursuit (changing fields or starting your own business), state this passion as a goal and chunk it out into benchmarks and hurdles. Don't worry if you can't map the entire path to this goal. Just focus on the first two or three benchmarks that you feel are achievable. Then reevaluate and extend your plan as you reach each benchmark.

The Goal: _____

_____

_____

Buy-In: Why do you want to achieve this goal?

_____

_____

_____

Achievability: Is your goal stated specifically enough? What is the total anticipated time commitment for achieving it?

_____

_____

_____

Positive Impact: How will you feel when you reach this goal? What impact will reaching it have on your life? What impact will it have on others?

_____

_____

_____

Complexity (Hurdles): What do you expect will get in your way of achieving this goal? What sacrifices do you expect you will have to make?

_____

_____

_____

Benchmarks: This is where you map out the individual steps you need to take to achieve your goal. Break down each benchmark with time commitments and smaller hurdles.

Benchmark Number 1: _____

ANTICIPATED TIME COMMITMENT TO REACH THIS BENCHMARK: _____

_____

EXPECTATIONS (HOW WILL I REACH THIS BENCHMARK?): _____

_____

_____

_____

HURDLES (SACRIFICES AND CHALLENGES I MAY ENCOUNTER AS I REACH FOR THIS BENCHMARK):

_____

_____

_____

CHECK-IN/PROGRESS NOTES: _____

_____

_____

_____

_____

Benchmark Number 2: _____

ANTICIPATED TIME COMMITMENT TO REACH THIS BENCHMARK: _____

_____

EXPECTATIONS (HOW WILL I REACH THIS BENCHMARK?): _____

_____

_____

_____

_____

HURDLES (SACRIFICES AND CHALLENGES I MAY ENCOUNTER AS I REACH FOR THIS BENCHMARK):

_____

_____

_____

_____

CHECK-IN/PROGRESS NOTES: _____

_____

_____

_____

Benchmark Number 3: _____

ANTICIPATED TIME COMMITMENT TO REACH THIS BENCHMARK: _____

_____

EXPECTATIONS (HOW WILL I REACH THIS BENCHMARK?): _____

_____

_____

_____

_____

HURDLES (SACRIFICES AND CHALLENGES I MAY ENCOUNTER AS I REACH FOR THIS BENCHMARK):

_____

_____

_____

_____

CHECK-IN/PROGRESS NOTES: _____

_____

_____

_____

Benchmark Number 4: _____

ANTICIPATED TIME COMMITMENT TO REACH THIS BENCHMARK: _____

_____

EXPECTATIONS (HOW WILL I REACH THIS BENCHMARK?): _____

_____

_____

_____

_____

HURDLES (SACRIFICES AND CHALLENGES I MAY ENCOUNTER AS I REACH FOR THIS BENCHMARK):

_____

_____

_____

CHECK-IN / PROGRESS NOTES: _____

_____

_____

_____

Before You Quit Your Day Job

Transitioning from a dream to real life requires action. You may have your sights set on the heavens, but you need to be grounded in reality. One thing to consider: Are your finances nimble enough to accommodate this sort of shift? It's an important question. You may be driven to let your passion subsume your work life, but if you are unable to make ends meet while you're in transition, the entire process has the potential to be very stressful. Here are a few suggestions for smoothing the ride.

1. Weigh the financial variables: There are more than you may be thinking about. Will you need extra schooling and training? Who will pay for your health care or match contributions to your retirement account? If you expect you will be in belt-tightening mode for a bit, how long will that period last? Knowing this is key to keeping your spending in check for as long as you'll need to. If you haven't mapped out all of the costs of quitting your current job or pursuing a new venture (whether it's starting your own business or going back to school), start brainstorming here:

_____

_____

_____

_____

_____

_____

_____

_____

_____

2. Trim your debts: You won't take much psychic pleasure in your new life if your old mortgage payment is stressing you out every month. Brainstorm some things that you could downsize. Keep your old, paid-off car rather than saddling yourself with a new monthly payment. And keep the credit cards at arm's length.

_____

_____

_____

_____

_____

_____

_____

_____

_____

3. Take a test-drive: Pretend you're living on a reduced income for several months to see if you can actually swing it. Once you figure out how much your cash flow will be compromised, create a new budget using the worksheet on page 16 (there are extras in the back of the journal). Sustain this experiment for as long as you can and bank everything that you save (this will beef up your emergency stash).

4. Explore Plan B: Inject More Passion into Your Current Work: There is, of course, a downside to finding your passion and then transitioning to pursue it. It takes time. Perhaps considerable time. So here's an alternative—and it's one to consider even if you are aiming to make that bigger transition in the long term: Learn to love what you do. This next series of exercises will tell you how.

Forge a Personal Connection with Your Boss

Try injecting more passion into your career by going to the one person who has the most immediate effect on your day-to-day work: your boss. If you're working for someone you feel is charismatic or inspirational, you're likely to want to perform better in that person's eyes. Schedule a breakfast meeting with your supervisor.

Jot down what you know about your boss's priorities and vision for the department. How might you, in your current role, participate more in fulfilling his or her vision? Prepare some questions to ask when you meet.

_____

_____

_____

_____

_____

_____

_____

_____

_____

_____

_____

_____

_____

_____

_____

_____

NOTE: For more ideas and exercises to help you boost your visibility and connections within your workplace, be sure to complete chapter 6, "Attribute Focus: Connectedness," beginning on page 89.

Find Autonomy in Your Job

Autonomy is key to feeling good about the work you do, no matter what kind of work it is. According to one study, hospital janitors who felt a calling went above and beyond their job descriptions. They interacted with patients and asked how they were feeling. They refilled water glasses. Nobody told them to do these things, but nobody told them not to, either. In other words, striking out for independence doesn't have to be a battle cry; it can be a whisper and have the same mood-elevating results.

Rewrite the way you think about four responsibilities associated with your job. Think about even the most menial tasks and recast them in a more significant light.

Task	Recasted Responsibility
I clean eighteen hospital rooms.	*I make sure that thirty-two patients are recovering in a clean and comfortable environment.*
1.	1.
2.	2.
3.	3.
4.	4.

Change Jobs, Not Careers

If you've tried everything and you're still not able to find some on-the-job satisfaction, the problem may be with the organization, not with you. Use the space in the first column of the chart below to write down five aspects of your current work environment that interfere with your job satisfaction. In the second column, jot down a situation that you would prefer.

Issue with My Current Company	Situation That I Would Prefer
There are too many middle managers with undefined authority.	*To work for one manager who has clear access to the top decision maker.*
1.	**1.**
2.	**2.**
3.	**3.**
4.	**4.**
5.	**5.**

NOTE: Use the exercises in chapter 6, "Attribute Focus: Connectedness" to start networking for a position in an organization (or a department within your own company) that fits the criteria in your chart.

Visualize the Next Logical Step

Whether you're finding the work you love or loving the work you do, it will help if you can visualize what comes next. So every day for the next week, take fifteen minutes out of your day to consider what you want next. It should be a fifteen-minute period when your brain is at its best. Sit down with this journal and imagine what's possible.

DAY 1 (date: _____/_____/_____)

_____

_____

_____

_____

_____

_____

_____

DAY 2 (date: _____/_____/_____)

_____

_____

_____

_____

_____

_____

_____

DAY 3 (date: _____/_____/_____)

_____

_____

_____

_____

_____

_____

DAY 4 (date: _____/_____/_____)

_____

_____

_____

_____

_____

_____

DAY 5 (date: _____/_____/_____)

_____

_____

_____

_____

_____

_____

DAY 6 (date: _____/_____/_____)

_____

_____

_____

_____

_____

_____

DAY 7 (date: _____/_____/_____)

_____

_____

_____

_____

_____

_____

EXERCISE

Visualize the Next Logical Step, Part Two

Go back and look at your daily notes and make one complete list of possible next steps on a separate sheet of paper. Once you have your short list, rate your ideas on a scale of 1 to 10 on these two criteria.

1. Can you own this idea? Is it something you could implement—on a small scale or a big one—and get credit for it?

2. Can you prosper from it? No, it's not all about the money. But money is a barometer of success and achievement. And if this next logical step will bring some your way, it's another way for you to feel rewarded.

Coming Up

Even if you are driven, hardworking, and passionate about what you do, there will always be a barrier between you and your dreams if you try to pursue them on your own. Hillary Clinton says, "It takes a village," and whether it comes to raising a child or getting rich—she's absolutely right. The wealthy are more connected and more social than those who are not. And they use their networks to help them get to the top and then stay there. In the next chapter, you'll learn that you likely have more connections than you think. I'll help you explore and exploit them, and we'll discuss why these social skills are as necessary in business as they are in personal life.

CHAPTER
N.º

ATTRIBUTE FOCUS:
CONNECTEDNESS

Date that I began this chapter: _____/_____/_____

Date that I completed this chapter: _____/_____/_____

We've all seen people move up the rungs of success from time to time and whispered (sometimes less than kindly): "Connections." They're not imagined, and they're proven to work.

People with the right kind of links to others can—if they know what they're doing—use those links to get noticed, get promotions, and get raises, all faster than if they were going it alone. In this chapter, you'll find exercises for breaking out of your shell and making connections that will benefit your career. This chapter will be particularly helpful if you are currently job hunting or looking to get promoted within your company.

Exercise Checklist
❏ Do You Have Enough Support?
❏ Find a Mentor
❏ Increase Your Visibility
❏ Get in Touch with Your Inner Values

Why It Pays to Be Connected
Connections matter. One 1988 study of managers found that the most successful spent 70 percent more time networking and 10 percent more time in routine communication (back then, this meant talking on the phone) than their less successful counterparts. Being well liked or popular matters. And so does having a support network. Our study asked that question a number of ways.

"I AM VERY SATISFIED WITH MY SOCIAL LIFE."	PERCENT THAT AGREED
Wealthy	46 percent
Financially comfortable	38 percent
Paycheck-to-paychecks	24 percent
Further-in-debtors	13 percent

"I AM VERY SATISFIED WITH MY COMMUNITY."	PERCENT THAT AGREED
Wealthy	40 percent
Financially comfortable	33 percent
Paycheck-to-paychecks	21 percent
Further-in-debtors	11 percent

"I WOULD SAY THAT I AM POPULAR."	PERCENT THAT AGREED
Wealthy	45 percent
Financially comfortable	24 percent
Paycheck-to-paychecks	17 percent
Further-in-debtors	17 percent

Interestingly, the range of people with whom the wealthy and financially comfortable socialize is much wider than average. Paycheck-to-paychecks and further-in-debtors are more likely to stick to their families; those doing well certainly spend time with their families but also enjoy the company of others who share their interests, neighbors, coworkers, and people who could help them advance financially or in their careers.

Social capital is the currency of connections. Like stocks, real estate, or other assets, social capital has value—sometimes huge value. But you may not be able to measure it in dollars and cents. Its currencies are information, resources, and sponsorship (when someone puts his or her neck out to further your career or help you in some other way). Social capital can net you promotions, jumps in salary, helpful contacts for the future and—often just as important—satisfaction.

But What If You're Not an Extrovert?

Woody Allen was only partially correct when he said 80 percent of success was showing up. You not only have to be there—you have to be there and then you have to get involved with people. "What you need to do is allow people to see that you're competent, as well as a nice and good person," explains Monica Forret, professor of business at St. Ambrose University, who started studying networking after noting that some people are really good at it, while others are not. People who were raised in higher socioeconomic households tend to have an edge, she says, not because they're more outgoing necessarily, but because they've seen this sort of behavior all their lives.

If your parents know people in positions of power, then chances are you do as well. The introductions have been made. But even if you haven't got those chits in your back pocket, this is a skill you can learn.

Cast a Net

Interestingly, researchers have found that a person doesn't have to be your best friend for that connection to provide a significant payoff. Weak ties in the workforce can be more valuable.

A weak tie is formed when you are both connected to a third person—a friend of a friend—or connected to a network in common—such as an alumni association. These weak ties have been shown to be the most important source of information about jobs; they can help in boosting salary, promotions, career satisfaction, and access to information. When it comes to those weak ties, more is better, so cast a wide net.

EXERCISE
Date: ____/____/____

Do You Have Enough Support?

Do you have enough people in your circle? Do you have the support you need to get ahead? Think back to the last time you had a problem, a real issue. It could be a problem you faced at work. It could be a problem you faced at home. Then answer the questions below based on the following scale:

0 = **Not at all**
1 = **To some degree**
2 = **Neutral**
3 = **To a large degree**
4 = **Completely**

1. How much did the primary person/most important people in your life give you advice or information about that problem (whether you wanted it or not)?	
2. How much did that person/those people help you with things related to your problem (for example, taking other items off your plate so you could focus or helping you find the right sources of information/additional support)?	

3. How much did that person/those people give you reassurance, encouragement, and emotional support (affection) concerning your problem?	
4. How much did that person/those people listen to and try to understand your worries about your problem?	
5. How much can you relax and be yourself around that person/those people?	
6. How much can you open up to that person/those people if you need to talk about your worries about your problem?	
7. How often does that person/those people argue with you relating to your problem?	
8. How often does that person/those people criticize you relating to your problem?	
9. How often does that person/those people let you down when you are counting on him/her/them?	
10. How often does that person/those people withdraw from discussions about your problem or try to change the topic away from your problem?	
TOTAL	

TO SCORE: For questions 1 through 6, simply add up the numbers. Score questions 7 through 10 in reverse (4 = 0; 3 = 1; 2 = 2; 1 = 3; 0 = 4). Then add up the numbers.

INTERPRETING YOUR SCORE: The highest score is 40.

At 30 and above, you have a decent amount of support in your life.

At 20 and above, you have a moderate amount, but you feel that more would be beneficial.

Below 20, this is an area where you could use some work.

I know that sounds strange, to say *you* need work. After all, we are looking at the behavior of others—behaviors that are not in your control. But the truth is, those other people are reacting to the energy, feelings, and effort you put out to them. By altering your own behaviors, you can influence those that come back to you. You can control whether people have a positive or negative experience in your presence. And that makes all The Difference in the world.

Find a Mentor

A mentor is a person higher up in your company or industry who can serve as a role model, providing the sort of counseling, friendship, honest feedback, and sometimes direct assistance that can help you get ahead. Studies show that people who receive more mentoring throughout their careers draw higher salaries, receive more promotions, and are more satisfied with their life's work overall.

Spend any time in the workforce, though, and you'll notice some people find mentors, and others don't. How do you make yourself one of the chosen?

TAKE INITIATIVE. Mentors tend to select protégés who seek them out. If you're looking for a mentor, you'll need to take the initiative, start conversations, build a relationship, and ask for what you want.

START BY ASKING FOR ADVICE. Once you've found someone who is highly respected, don't come out and ask, "Will you be my mentor?" Say hello a couple of times. Then ask him or her, "I'm wondering if we can get together for coffee or lunch. I'd like to get some advice or support." Asking for advice is preferable to asking for help for two reasons. First, it's flattering. When you ask someone for advice you're showing them you value their knowledge. Second, advice doesn't require the person you're connecting with to ask anything of someone else. It's easier to offer and doesn't require the expenditure of any of that person's social capital.

ESTABLISH COMMON GROUND. Keep in mind that mentors gravitate toward protégés with whom they have something in common—such as social status or upbringing—or people who remind them of themselves when they were younger.

MULTIPLY YOUR EFFORTS. Newer research suggests that having multiple mentors is better than finding one person to help you along the way. Why? Because no one mentor may be able to help with all your work/life challenges.

NOTE: Follow up. If someone offers you help, take them up on it. The very next day, place a call or send an e-mail expressing your gratitude. That will ensure that your new connection does as promised, and by following up so quickly you're signaling how much you value their help or advice.

Are there a few people in your company whom you admire? Brainstorm how you might approach each one for advice, then come back and jot down his or her feedback. Who seemed the most receptive? Did you discover anything that you have in common?

_____

_____

_____

_____

_____

_____

_____

_____

_____

_____

_____

_____

_____

_____

_____

_____

_____

_____

_____

Increase Your Visibility

Being visible means connecting with people in your organization who are outside your own function or area, preferably at a higher pay grade. Increasing your visibility can lead to more promotions and higher compensation. If you're looking to work your way up the corporate ladder, maybe you should join something social at work—the AIDS or breast cancer walk team, for example—to let people see you in another light.

Make a list of activities that will connect you with other people in your company. Understand that joining isn't enough. Ideally, you'll want to find your way into a leadership role. That means figuring out which committees are the most meaningful and valued and then volunteering for them.

_____

_____

_____

_____

_____

_____

_____

_____

_____

_____

_____

_____

_____

_____

EXERCISE

Get in Touch with Your Inner Values

Research has shown that writing about values of personal importance to you can help you look at the world outwardly rather than inwardly. In one experiment, conducted by University of Michigan psychologist Jennifer Crocker and her colleagues, students were asked to rank the following values in order of personal importance:

Business	Science/pursuit of knowledge
Art/music/theater	Religion/morality
Social life/relationships	Government/politics

Some of the students were then asked to spend ten minutes writing about the value that was most important to them. Afterward, those same students were asked to rate "how much they felt" eighteen feelings, including love, connectedness, empathy, pride, power, weakness, and defensiveness.

No matter which value the students chose as the most important, writing about it increased their feelings of love and connectedness—and decreased feelings of defensiveness. In other words, it provided a boost to self-esteem that made these students more immune to the pressures of the outside world.

Why does this work? The writing exercise helps you escape your boundaries by reminding you what you care about other than yourself. Feeling loved and connected may also dampen your defenses so that you can take in information that, while useful, may otherwise be hard or threatening to take in: on-the-job criticism, for example, or a spouse's nudge to do something differently.

Now you try it: Take ten minutes and write about the value that is most important to you (choose one from the list above and follow the prompts on the next page). Note how you feel at the end. Are you less agitated? Feel safer? More secure? If so, it's working. A week later, do the exercise again.

NOTE: If this is an exercise you don't have time for on a regular basis, you may want to use it before you face, say, your next performance review. It's helpful in any situation where the information is difficult or you find yourself losing track of what's really important.

WEEK 1 (date: ___/___/___)

I VALUE: _____

Why is this important? What about it do I value?

_____
_____
_____
_____
_____
_____
_____
_____
_____
_____
_____
_____
_____

My state of mind after writing this (Less agitated? Feel safer? More secure?):

_____
_____
_____
_____

WEEK 2 (date: ____/____/____)

I VALUE: _____

Why is this important? What about it do I value?

_____

_____

_____

_____

_____

_____

_____

_____

_____

_____

_____

_____

_____

My state of mind after writing this (Less agitated? Feel safer? More secure?):

_____

_____

_____

_____

Coming Up

We started to address the topic of happiness and optimism in the preceding exercise, and now we're going to tackle it head-on. In the next chapter, you'll learn how much happiness is optimal for success, as well as how to increase your optimism quotient.

CHAPTER
Nọ

7

ATTRIBUTE FOCUS:

OPTIMISM

Date that I began this chapter: _____/_____/_____

Date that I completed this chapter: _____/_____/_____

Some people believe that money leads to happiness. Reverse this, however, and you've a much stronger case. Happiness—without a doubt—leads to money and success. Likewise, so does optimism.

A happy and optimistic state of mind enables you to solve problems, conjure ideas, take long-range consequences into consideration, and come back and try again if you miss the first time. You don't want to be overly happy or overly optimistic, though—that can lead to a loss of competitive juices that are helpful in making The Difference a part of your life. In this chapter, you'll learn what separates happiness from optimism, and try a few exercises that will help you attain the right amounts of each. Perhaps more than any of the other attributes explored in my research, happiness and optimism have direct links to all the others. They make the most "difference."

Exercise Checklist
❏ **The Life Orientation Test**
❏ **Compare and Contrast Favorably**
❏ **Learn to Savor: Write Three Good Things About Each Day**
❏ **Write About the Very Best You**

Get Happy (but Not Too Happy)
Clearly happiness is something we feel is worth striving for, at least by measuring the number of books sold on the subject. And with good reason. Happy people are more likely to achieve their goals because, the research tells us, it's easier to make progress toward those goals when you're in a good frame of mind. And—for a whole litany of reasons—happy people are more successful. (They tend to be more productive, more creative, and more dependable, and they produce higher quality work. They get promoted and their salaries rise accordingly.)

In other words, although wealth cannot buy you happiness, happiness does seem to be able to buy you money. The connection is apparent when you look specifically at our research.

ARE YOU HAPPY?	PERCENT THAT ANSWERED "YES"
Wealthy	55 percent
Financially comfortable	56 percent
Paycheck-to-paychecks	39 percent
Further-in-debtors	32 percent

Happiness and Optimism Are Not the Same Thing

Happiness is what you're feeling today about how things are going in the short and long term. Academics refer to it as your sense of well-being. Optimism is a way of looking at the future. It's a tendency to believe you'll experience good rather than bad outcomes in life. It's the expectation that good things are going to be plentiful.

In short, happiness is about today. Optimism is about tomorrow.

ARE YOU OPTIMISTIC?	PERCENT THAT ANSWERED "YES"
Wealthy	56 percent
Financially comfortable	54 percent
Paycheck-to-paychecks	40 percent
Further-in-debtors	31 percent

When It Comes to Your Money, You Want to Be Both Optimistic and Happy . . .

Like happy people, optimists do well financially. They also do well on the job. Optimists work more hours and they expect to retire later in life (and thus build up bigger retirement stashes). Optimists save more, keep more of their wealth in liquid assets, invest more in individual stocks, and are more likely to pay their credit card bills promptly. And when optimists divorce they are more likely than pessimists to remarry. Even that is good for wealth.

But Not Too Optimistic or Happy

What you don't want to be—it turns out—is a sap.

One factor at work here is a hidden con of happiness. Although it's true that positive emotions tend to make you more expansive and more creative, they also make you rely on tried-and-true answers. As long as your internal problem-solving methodology is working, why would you try anything new? The down-side is that when that approach stops working, you may not recognize it.

In other words, the emotional system is a little like a gas gauge. You want it to work. But you don't want it to be on full or empty all the time. You want it to register that there's a bear chasing you, so that you'll be afraid and run a little faster. But you don't want it to shoot to the top with every little cricket on your tail. A properly working emotional system is your ally. You want to spend your time and energy on those things that are potentially major prob-lems. But if you find yourself dwelling on the paper clips or the small mis-takes, you'll never get anything done.

As you've worked through this journal, you've probably found that the boundaries that separate some of the elements that make up The Difference are a bit, well, squishy. One attribute tends to beget the next, which leads to another, which happens to be tied to the first one. This is truer of optimism and happiness than perhaps any of the others.

EXERCISE

Date: ____/____/____

The Life Orientation Test—Revised

So, where do you stack up? Are you too optimistic or not optimistic enough? Academics have been using the Life Orientation Test to measure optimism for the past few decades. This is the revised version.

Write a number next to each statement that indicates the extent to which you agree or disagree with that statement based on the following scale. Be as honest and accurate as you can throughout. Try not to let your response to one statement influence your responses to other statements. There are no "correct" or "incorrect" answers. Answer according to your own feelings, rather than how you think "most people" would answer.

0 = **Strongly Disagree**

1 = **Disagree**

2 = **You are neutral about the statement**

3 = **Agree**

4 = **Strongly Agree**

1.	In uncertain times, I would expect the best.	
2.	It's easy for me to relax.	
3.	If something can go wrong with me, it will.	
4.	I am always optimistic about my future.	
5.	I enjoy my friends a lot.	
6.	It's important for me to keep busy.	
7.	I hardly ever expect things to go my way.	
8.	I don't get upset too easily.	
9.	I rarely count on good things happening to me.	
10.	Overall, I expect more good things to happen to me than bad.	
	TOTAL	

TO SCORE: Items 2, 5, 6, and 8 are fillers. Don't count them at all. For numbers 1, 4, and 10, simply add up the numbers. Score numbers 3, 7, and 9 in reverse (0 = 4; 1 = 3; 2 = 2; 3 = 1; 4 = 0.) Then add up your numbers.

INTERPRETING YOUR SCORE: The highest possible score is 24. The higher your score, the more optimistic you are with a breakdown that looks roughly like this:

At 20 or above, you are optimistic.

At 14 to 19, you are mildly optimistic.

At 11 to 13, you are neutral.

At 6 to 10, you are mildly pessimistic.

At 5 or under, you are pessimistic.

What If You're Not Happy or Optimistic Enough?

You may be looking at these results and thinking: "So what? I was born this way. There is nothing I can do about it." That is decidedly untrue. Only about 50 percent of optimism and happiness is innate. What's more, starting from nothing can mean you'll see bigger improvements than if you start from so-so. The lower you are on the scale, the more improvements mean (that is, a grumpy person who becomes moderately happy is likely to see a bigger boost in income than a happy person who becomes happier). So—moderate!

Compare and Contrast Favorably

We all compare ourselves to others. It's the American thing to do. One tool that you can use to build your sense of optimism is to think about a few areas where you consistently catch yourself "comparing down" (that is, comparing yourself to others and feeling that you don't measure up). Rather than casting yourself and your accomplishments in a negative light, choose your comparative set so that you come out looking good. This will be hard at first, but over time, it will become second nature. Use this chart to rewrite five statements about yourself.

Comparing Down	Comparing Favorably
I'm the least flexible one in my yoga class.	*I'm the most flexible one in the class among the beginners.*
1.	1.
2.	2.
3.	3.
4.	4.
5.	5.

Learn to Savor

Small positive things happen every day. (Good weather, a nice painting on the wall, the fact that today's office coffee is better than the usual sludge: These are all small, positive things.) The goal is to learn to be present and start to notice the good things that are happening around you. Start small: Taste your hamburger, don't just eat it. You don't have to stop what you're doing, just be mindful of your actions. Savor the beauty of the moment. **Once a day for two weeks, take a few minutes to note three good things about your day.**

DAY 1 (date: _____/_____/_____)

1. _____

2. _____

3. _____

DAY 2 (date: _____/_____/_____)

1. _____

2. _____

3. _____

DAY 3 (date: _____/_____/_____)

1. _____

2. _____

3. _____

DAY 4 (date: _____/_____/_____)

1. _____

2. _____

3. _____

DAY 5 (date: ____/____/____)

1. _____

2. _____

3. _____

DAY 6 (date: ____/____/____)

1. _____

2. _____

3. _____

DAY 7 (date: ____/____/____)

1. _____

2. _____

3. _____

DAY 8 (date: ____/____/____)

1. _____

2. _____

3. _____

DAY 9 (date: ____/____/____)

1. _____

2. _____

3. _____

DAY 10 (date: _____/_____/_____)

1. _____

2. _____

3. _____

DAY 11 (date: _____/_____/_____)

1. _____

2. _____

3. _____

DAY 12 (date: _____/_____/_____)

1. _____

2. _____

3. _____

DAY 13 (date: _____/_____/_____)

1. _____

2. _____

3. _____

DAY 14 (date: _____/_____/_____)

1. _____

2. _____

3. _____

Evaluating the Three Good Things

Look back over the past two weeks. Some good things just "happen," and others are things that you can make happen, or at least encourage through your own actions. In general, you'll start to feel more optimistic if you can make a link between your own behavior and a positive outcome.

Use this page to think about how you might encourage the good things on your lists to happen again.

_____

_____

_____

_____

_____

_____

_____

_____

_____

_____

_____

_____

_____

_____

Write About the Very Best You

Research has shown that thinking about your life in the future in the best possible terms is likely to have a good influence on the decisions that you make now, as well as on your current outlook on life. Consider the very best version of yourself. What have you accomplished and how did you get here? What would your ideal life look like in the future if you could spell it out for yourself? Try this exercise at least twice.

As you go through the process, use positive terms (instead of negative ones) to explain your actions. Don't write: "I can't afford to live in the city so I live in the suburbs." Write: "I live in the suburbs rather than the city because I choose to spend my money on other things." Remember, on these pages you are not a victim, you are in charge. To help get you going, start out by filling in the following blanks.

Today I am: _____

_____

_____

_____

I got here by: _____

_____

_____

Five years from now I will be: _____

_____

_____

_____

I got here by: _____

_____

Ten years from now I will be: _____

_____

_____

_____

I got here by: _____

_____

_____

_____

Twenty years from now I will be: _____

_____

_____

_____

I got here by: _____

_____

_____

_____

I am most proud of: _____

_____

_____

_____

_____

_____

Coming Up

If you're starting to feel more optimistic that things can go your way, the next chapter will teach you how to recover when a plan, an investment, or anything else in life backfires. The Donald Trumps of the world will tell you, it's not so much that they're able to get ahead— it's that when they get clobbered (and successful, wealthy people inevitably do at one time or another) they're able to dust themselves off and succeed again. It's not ambition so much as it's resilience. And it's one of the most important components of The Difference.

CHAPTER
№
8

ATTRIBUTE FOCUS:
RESILIENCE

Date that I began this section: _____/_____/_____

Date that I completed this section: _____/_____/_____

Why is it that some people seem to be able to rebound so much more quickly than others? It's called resilience. And it's a key element in The Difference. And even if what doesn't kill you doesn't necessarily make you stronger, it does seem to give you a leg up on wealth.

The exercises in this chapter are designed to build your resilience, your ability to pick yourself up and start all over again. You'll take a test to learn where your greatest coping skills lie—and then use that information to help you sharpen and beef up your weaknesses. The rest of the exercises should be completed as negative situations come up in your life. Come back to this chapter when you need to and check off the exercises as you try them.

Exercise Checklist
❑ How Do You Cope?
❑ Finding Control
❑ Do Something
❑ Find a Cheerleader
❑ Recast Your Experiences
❑ Put It in Perspective

In Praise of the Do-Over
Things happen. S—t happens.

So what can you do? You can cave in to these events, some of which you can control a little, some of which you can't control at all. Or you can learn to deal, to ride it out, to come to terms with the fact that the other things will take care of themselves in time.

This is called resilience. It's not a new word, by any means, but it does seem to have been reinvigorated lately by both the media and academics. This makes sense, considering the definition, which, according to Merriam-Webster, is "the ability to recover from or adjust easily to misfortune or change." That sounds like a dose of precisely what we need right now.

Resilient people have the ability to keep moving forward—to avoid getting stuck in some pool of negativity. They don't deny the bad things that happen in all of our lives, but they're able to focus on things they can control with the belief that they have the ability to effect change.

People who know The Difference are resilient, as our data shows.

"I CAN OVERCOME A BAD SITUATION."	PERCENT THAT AGREED
Wealthy	49 percent
Financially comfortable	51 percent
Paycheck-to-paychecks	40 percent
Further-in-debtors	37 percent

Increasing Your RQ (Resilience Quotient)

This is the chapter you will come back to whenever you encounter a set-back of any kind (financial or otherwise). Each exercise provides a different strategy for improving your ability to cope. Some will fit the way you see the world, and you'll be able to incorporate them into your thinking. Others may seem so straightforward you can cross them off your list; these are things you do already. And, finally, there will be those that—to you—are akin to an orange sweater (and you don't wear orange) or steak tartare (and you like your meat well done). That's okay, too. Not all strategies work for all people; that's why I've tried to acknowledge that so many exist.

If you don't complete any of this chapter's other exercises at this time, at least pause to take the "How Do You Cope?" evaluation below.

What Happens When You Learn These Skills?

Resilient people have the ability to take the appropriate risks necessary to embrace The Difference. They're more comfortable in uncomfortable situations. They can overcome pessimism. They can pull themselves out of minor depressions.

Why? Because resilience—learned resilience—gives humans the power to overcome our innate negativity. We appear to be hardwired to pay more attention to the bad things that happen than the good things. When people hunt the good stuff, it increases positive emotions, and that improves resilience. Think of it as filling up your positivity tank so that you have enough power to keep going when you're under stress and need it most.

How Do You Cope?

That's the first question. We do it in different ways at different times. Psychologist Charles S. Carver of the University of Miami has designed a diagnostic called COPE. What follows is his brief version edited slightly for these purposes.

Write a number next to each statement below based on the following scale. As you go through the questions, answer them quickly and honestly, paying close attention to what extent you've been doing what the item says. You want to gauge how often or how much you've been doing this, not whether it seems to be working for you. Try to approach each question individually. At the end, you'll see which coping mechanisms you use well and where you need work.

1 = I haven't been doing this at all
2 = I've been doing this a little bit
3 = I've been doing this a medium amount
4 = I've been doing this a lot

1. I've been turning to work or other activities to take my mind off things.	
2. I've been concentrating my efforts on doing something about the situation I'm in.	
3. I've been saying to myself, "This isn't real."	
4. I've been using alcohol or other drugs to make myself feel better.	
5. I've been getting emotional support from others.	
6. I've given up trying to deal with it.	
7. I've been taking action to try to make the situation better.	
8. I've been refusing to believe that it has happened.	
9. I've been saying things to let my unpleasant feelings escape.	
10. I've been getting help and advice from other people.	
11. I've been using alcohol or other drugs to help me get through it.	
12. I've been trying to see it in a different light—to make it seem more positive.	

13. I've been criticizing myself.	
14. I've been trying to come up with a strategy about what to do.	
15. I've been getting comfort and understanding from someone.	
16. I've given up the attempt to cope.	
17. I've been looking for something good in what is happening.	
18. I've been making jokes about it.	
19. I've been doing something to think about it less, such as going to movies, watching TV, reading, daydreaming, sleeping, or shopping.	
20. I've been accepting the reality of the fact that it has happened.	
21. I've been expressing my negative feelings.	
22. I've been trying to find comfort in my religion or spiritual beliefs.	
23. I've been trying to get advice or help from other people about what to do.	
24. I've been learning to live with it.	
25. I've been thinking hard about what steps to take.	
26. I've been blaming myself for things that happened.	
27. I've been praying or meditating.	
28. I've been making fun of the situation.	
TOTAL	

SCORING: Unfortunately, you can't add up your scores on this test and use the final tally as a definitive measure of whether you're resilient or not. Use the following key to figure out which coping measures you're using a lot and which ones you're not.

Self-distraction 1, 19

Active coping 2, 7

Denial 3, 8

Substance use 4, 11

Use of emotional support 5, 15

Use of instrumental support 10, 23

Behavioral disengagement 6, 16

Venting 9, 21

Positive reframing 12, 17

Planning 14, 25

Humor 18, 28

Acceptance 20, 24

Spirituality or religion 22, 27

Self-blame 13, 26

Finding Control

Ask yourself one question: Do I have to change or does someone else have to change for me to overcome a problem? Resilient people are able to identify and then focus on the things they can control, rather than trying to change things they cannot. For example, you cannot control (or predict, but that's another story) whether the stock market goes up or down on a particular day, week, month, or year. But you can control how much you decide to put in stocks rather than bonds, how seriously you take asset allocation and diversification, whether you decide to look at your portfolio on a daily, weekly, or even quarterly basis, and how you respond to it when you do. Apply this way of thinking to one of your own problems, below:

Today my frustration/setback/concern is: _____

_____

_____

_____

I have no control over these aspects of the situation: _____

_____

_____

_____

_____

These are things that I can control or do to alleviate stress: _____

_____

_____

_____

_____

Do Something

If you're dwelling on the negative you may not be trying to solve your problems because you don't know where to start. Brainstorm two or three possible solutions to a problem, then pick one. And go about implementing it. Just like exercising frees your mind to explore other options, taking action when you're stuck—even if it's a wrongheaded, inefficient action—can get you moving. After you've taken your first stab, come back to this page and write about what worked or didn't work out for you.

Today, my frustration/setback/concern is: _____

_____

_____

_____

_____

None of these is perfect, but three possible solutions to this problem are:

1. _____

2. _____

3. _____

CHECKING BACK IN:

I tried solution number _____ **and here's how it worked out:**

_____

_____

_____

_____

_____

Find a Cheerleader

Linda Meccouri, a professor at Springfield Technical Community College in Massachusetts, says, "This Horatio Alger story, that you can raise yourself up by your bootstraps, is a myth." Meccouri has spent the last twenty-six years taking oral histories of people, primarily women, who have escaped poverty and found financial comfort, and she says her subjects—to a one—have said, "There's a person in my life. An ally. A mentor." Use the questions below to find someone who can mentor you through a current difficulty.

My current frustration/setback/concern is: _____

_____

1. Someone in my life who can offer support and comfort: _____

_____

2. Someone in my life who has been in a similar situation: _____

_____

_____

CHECKING BACK IN:

Here's who I sought out for advice/support and some feedback that I received:

_____

_____

_____

_____

_____

_____

Learn to Recast Your Experiences

New research is telling us that it's better for our resilience to make sure that when we retell our life stories we do it in such a way that it bolsters our confidence rather than weakens it. How do you do that?

Write about your current frustration or setback in the third person. Doing it this way gives you the ability to step back and be impartial and allows you to figure out why you behaved and felt as you did. Pay attention to whether you make it seem like things happened to you or whether you made things happen. The former tends to victimize you, the latter makes you stronger.

_____

_____

_____

_____

_____

_____

_____

_____

_____

_____

_____

_____

_____

_____

Now look at the negatives. If you gloss over the unpleasant experiences in your retelling, you don't give yourself the opportunity to learn from them. Delve into them in a detailed way. How are you in a better place because you went through these challenges? You may not even recognize these hidden benefits until you explain them on this page.

Put It in Perspective

When adversity strikes a nonresilient person, they will start to turn it into a catastrophe. The story might start, "If I can't pay my credit card bill this month," but the ending is cataclysmic: "the world stops spinning and nothing will be right ever, ever again." A resilient person can stop the madness.

This is a skill you can learn. Consider one of your current worries. Then write down your catastrophic beliefs. Then, challenge your worst-case scenario by constructing a fantastic best-case scenario. What you will start to see is that neither scenario is reality based. And now that you're loosened up, you can do the hard work and look at reality. Here's an example:

CURRENT WORRY: "I'm going to lose my job."

CATASTROPHE: "My girlfriend will dump me, my dog will hate me, I will end up eating Mickey-D's out of a Dumpster."

FANTASY: "Tomorrow, I'll discover the cure for cancer. Someone will give me my own talk show. I'll win the lottery even though I don't play."

REALITY: "I'm going to have to redo my resume. It'll probably take me three to four months to land something good."

NOW IT'S YOUR TURN:

Current worry: _____

_____

_____

_____

Catastrophe: _____

_____

_____

_____

_____

Fantasy: _____
_____
_____
_____

Reality: _____
_____
_____
_____

Coming Up

*In one of those clever American Express fill-in-the-blank ads, 30
Rock's Tina Fey is asked what she's most proud of. "That my
daughter says 'Please and thank you,'" she answers. Turns out she's
on to something. Gratitude—not just saying it, but feeling it and
believing it—is now tied to increased success, income, wealth, and a
whole host of other differentiating factors. In other words, karma's
kickback is alive and well and ready for you to learn its lesson . . .
in the final chapter of this journal.*

CHAPTER
№

9

ATTRIBUTE FOCUS:
GRATITUDE AND GIVING BACK

Date that I began this chapter: _____/_____/_____

Date that I completed this chapter: _____/_____/_____

INTRODUCTION

What does it mean to be grateful? It means, certainly, to feel thankful. But research argues that it is more than that. Gratitude can be a habit you practice like yoga; it can be an attribute—a part of your personality—like optimism; it can even be a moral code you adhere to in the same way that some people follow the Ten Commandments.

The exercises in this chapter are designed to build your sense of gratitude. Gratefulness is linked to almost every other element of The Difference—optimism, resilience, connectedness, and so on. And that makes this final chapter an important one to absorb.

Exercise Checklist
❏ How Grateful Are You?
❏ Set Up Visual Cues
❏ Start a Gratitude Journal

Grazie
First, let's look at the role gratitude plays in The Difference. Unlike some of the other words with which wealthy people self-identified, "grateful" did not stand out from the mix.

DOES "GRATEFUL" DESCRIBE YOU VERY WELL?	PERCENT THAT ANSWERED "YES"
Wealthy	60 percent
Financially comfortable	59 percent
Paycheck-to-paychecks	54 percent
Further-in-debtors	58 percent

That may be because unlike "optimistic" or "competitive" or other factors where there were as many as thirty percentage points separating the wealthy from the further-in-debtors, as with hard work (where there was only a five percentage point differential), it's hard to live in this country, where even those who have very little have so much, and confess you're not grateful.

We see greater differences when we look at gratitude from an action-oriented perspective. They showed up when we asked:

DOES THE STATEMENT "I GIVE BACK TO THE COMMUNITY AS MUCH AS I CAN" DESCRIBE YOU VERY WELL?	PERCENT THAT ANSWERED "YES"
Wealthy	35 percent
Financially comfortable	25 percent
Paycheck-to-paychecks	21 percent
Further-in-debtors	21 percent

Gratitude not only drives your wealth, it is tied to many other benefits—physical and emotional. Grateful people are happier and more optimistic. Grateful people are healthier. They sleep more and exercise more, and that puts them in a better frame of mind. Grateful people are less likely to have depression or stress-based ailments. And they are more likely to feel physically better in a general sense. One 2003 study that asked people to count their blessings on a weekly basis for ten weeks found that people who followed through reported simply feeling healthier.

Grateful people are more likely to be connected—in the way you want to be connected. They are more trusting of people they don't know, viewing others as having good or relatively good motives, rather than being suspicious. Grateful people are very good at giving a little every day. And because they often get a little in return, they don't feel empty—and need to fill that void with unnecessary belongings.

If you are grateful for what you have—if you thank the lord, the stars, your spouse, and your friends for the good things they bring to your life every day—there's less room to be envious of what the Joneses are bringing into their lives. Feeling grateful is perhaps the fastest way to feel richer.

THE DIFFERENCE
WEALTH-BUILDING JOURNAL

How Grateful Are You?

All of which raises the following question: How much gratitude do you have in your life? Robert A. Emmons, a professor of psychology at the University of California, Davis, and Michael E. McCullough, a professor of psychology and religious studies at the University of Miami, and their colleagues devised the following questionnaire. They call it the GQ-6. The researchers actually started with thirty-nine questions and winnowed them down to these six by noting, over time, which ones seemed to be the most accurate measuring tools. Here's how to take it.

Using the scale below as a guide, write a number beside each statement to indicate how much you agree with it.

1 = Strongly disagree

2 = Disagree

3 = Slightly disagree

4 = Neutral

5 = Slightly agree

6 = Agree

7 = Strongly agree

1. I have so much in life to be thankful for.	
2. If I had to list everything that I felt grateful for, it would be a very long list.	
3. When I look at the world, I don't see much to be grateful for.	
4. I am grateful to a wide variety of people.	
5. As I get older, I find myself more able to appreciate the people, events, and situations that have been part of my life history.	
6. Long amounts of time can go by before I feel grateful to something or someone.	
TOTAL	

TO SCORE: For questions 1, 2, 4, and 5, simply add up the numbers. Score questions 3 and 6 in reverse (7 = 1; 6 = 2; 5 = 3; 4 = 4; 3 = 5; 2 = 6; 1 = 7). Add up your numbers.

INTERPRETING YOUR SCORE: The highest score is 42.

At 35 or above, you are grateful.

Below 35, you need brushing up.

When McCullough recently gave the questionnaire to more than 1,200 individuals, the majority of people scored 35 or higher—with a sizable number scoring over 38. Of course, some of the same biases that showed up in our "hardworking" and "grateful" questions could be at play here as well. But if you find your score below that, and even if you're well within that range, learning some techniques to incorporate more gratitude into your daily life might make being grateful seem a little bit more natural.

EXERCISE

Date: ____/____/____

Set Up Visual Cues

I have a sign in my kitchen that says "The most important things in life aren't things." It is one of several in my house—another simply says "Breathe"—which I use to remind myself of what's important. Why is this necessary? Because there are days when the dog throws up, the garbage disposal goes on the fritz, the car won't start (because I left the overhead light on again, dammit!), and my hair looks like hell. And although none of those things really matters, every single one can throw me off kilter and make me forget to hug the kids on the way out the door.

Take the time to create some visual cues. It can be a list of things you're grateful for that you keep with you in your purse or wallet. Look through pictures that represent important people or wonderful memories and put them out where you can see them. Jot down some ideas here, and then follow through.

_____

_____

_____

_____

Start a Gratitude Journal

Gratitude journals are not new. But we are starting to see more of their benefits with each passing year. According to Emmons's research, individuals who keep gratitude journals sleep a half hour more per night than those who don't, they exercise one-third more each week than those who don't, they're 25 percent happier than those who don't, and they tend to become people magnets. Although keeping a journal is a private exercise, the people who journal become more enthusiastic and pleasant to be around during the process. Their relationships are more rewarding, and that leads to all kinds of successes.

Once a day for no more than five or ten minutes, systematically write about the things that you are grateful for and explain why you're grateful in as much detail as possible.

In the beginning, you'll likely focus on concrete tangible things—your car, apartment, iPod. Eventually, you'll see a gradual shift or evolution toward more intangibles. You'll start to think about relationships that you value and ways others have done things for your benefit. You may even find gratitude for life itself.

DAY 1 (date: ____/____/____)

I'm thankful for: _____

_____

_____

_____

_____

_____

_____

DAY 2 (date: _____/_____/_____)

I'm thankful for: _____

_____

_____

_____

_____

_____

DAY 3 (date: _____/_____/_____)

I'm thankful for: _____

_____

_____

_____

_____

_____

DAY 4 (date: _____/_____/_____)

I'm thankful for: _____

_____

_____

_____

_____

_____

DAY 5 (date: ____/____/____)

I'm thankful for: _____

_____

_____

_____

_____

_____

DAY 6 (date: ____/____/____)

I'm thankful for: _____

_____

_____

_____

_____

_____

DAY 7 (date: ____/____/____)

I'm thankful for: _____

_____

_____

_____

_____

_____

Conclusion: You May Want to Give Financially, as Well

There is—by the way—another financial tie to gratitude. Grateful people give more. They give more of their money, more of their time, and no doubt even more of their belongings into the sidewalk box for Goodwill or the Salvation Army. The trick is giving smart: making the biggest difference not just for your own psyche, but for the organization you're looking to serve as well. How do you know your money is going to the right cause?

LOOK AT THE PROGRAM RATIO—BUT NOT EXCLUSIVELY: Consult websites like CharityNavigator.org or look over the IRS Form 990 that the charity files (available at GuideStar.org or on the charity's site). Look for the line that says "program org. to program." The higher the program ratio, the better job a charity is doing deploying your money. It's a good initial barometer, but the ratio doesn't always show how effective a program is. A food bank, for example, may shell out a lot on its program, but how many people is it feeding?

COMPARE ORGANIZATIONS THAT HAVE SIMILAR MISSIONS: The worst food bank spends 90 cents of every dollar on its programs because, basically, there are no administrative costs. Yet it's rare to find a museum that spends more than 75 cents on the dollar because museums need guards, insurance, and big buildings. So look at how one food bank compares with another food bank, not how one food bank compares with a museum.

GIVE NEW ORGANIZATIONS A BREAK: Charities less than two or three years old shouldn't be evaluated on the basis of program ratios, because their start-up costs are overhead by definition. Consider other data hiding in plain sight. Revenue growth combined with growth in spending on programs from year to year signals a financially healthy organization.

GET PAST THE SALES PITCH: You want answers to questions such as: "What are this group's goals for the year?" and "How will it reach them?" Well-run organizations welcome those questions. If a program is aimed at reducing an area's high-school-dropout rate, has it worked? And how much did it cost to achieve that reduction?

BOTTOM LINE: THE IMPULSE TO GIVE COMES FROM THE HEART. But the actual giving? As you would with any investment, use your head.

Extra Budget Worksheets

EXPENSE	MONTH 1	MONTH 2	MONTH 3	MONTH 4
HOUSING				
Rent/mortgage				
Home-equity loan				
Heat				
Water				
Electricity				
Insurance				
Phone				
Internet				
Cable				
Lawn/garden				
Repairs				
Other services				
Percent of total **(Housing should represent 35%.)**				
TRANSPORTATION				
Car payment 1				
Car payment 2				
Gasoline				
Insurance				
Repairs/upkeep				
Commuting				
Parking				
Other				
Percent of total **(Transportation should represent 15%.)**				

EXPENSE	MONTH 1	MONTH 2	MONTH 3	MONTH 4
CREDIT CARDS / LOANS				
Credit card 1				
Credit card 2				
Credit card 3				
Credit card 4				
Other loan 1				
Other loan 2				
Other				
Percent of total **(Debt repayment should represent 15%.)**				
CHILD CARE				
Babysitting				
Tuition				
Clothing				
Lessons				
Toys				
Gifts				
Other				
FOOD				
Groceries				
Eating out				
Entertaining				
Other				
PERSONAL				
Clothing				
Beauty shop/barbershop				
Dry-cleaning				
Health club				

EXPENSE	MONTH 1	MONTH 2	MONTH 3	MONTH 4
Cell phone/BlackBerry				
Gifts				
Other				
MEDICAL				
Insurance				
Co-pays				
Prescriptions				
Unreimbursed medical				
ENTERTAINMENT				
Tickets (movies/theater/concert/sports)				
CDs/DVDs				
Books/magazines				
Other				
TRAVEL				
Vacation				
Other				
PETS				
Food				
Medical care				
Grooming				
Other				
OTHER				
Percent of total (All these categories combined should represent 25%.)				

EXPENSE	MONTH 1	MONTH 2	MONTH 3	MONTH 4
SAVINGS/INVESTMENTS				
401(k) contribution				
Other retirement contribution				
Monthly savings				
Percent of total (You're aiming to save 10%.)				
Total Anticipated Savings:				

Secure Your Financial Future Forever

Through candid interviews and a study of more than five thousand people, Jean Chatzky has identified the traits and habits of those who have moved from the lowest economic state to the highest. Read *The Difference: How Anyone Can Prosper in Even the Toughest Times* to learn more about her groundbreaking research.